How to Overcome Regret

CRAFTED BY SKRIUWER

Copyright © 2024 by Skriuwer.

All rights reserved. No part of this book may be used or reproduced in any form whatsoever without written permission except in the case of brief quotations in critical articles or reviews.

For more information, contact : **kontakt@skriuwer.com** (www.skriuwer.com)

TABLE OF CONTENTS

CHAPTER 1: UNDERSTANDING THE CONCEPT OF REGRET

- *How regret differs from guilt or shame*
- *Why regret can linger and affect daily life*
- *Initial strategies to shift from regret to insight*

CHAPTER 2: HOW REGRET DEVELOPS OVER TIME

- *Small decisions that grow into larger remorse*
- *Memory distortion and social influences on regret*
- *Practical ways to address regret early*

CHAPTER 3: THE INFLUENCE OF THOUGHT PATTERNS ON REGRET

- *Spotting negative filters and "if only" loops*
- *Replacing harmful self-talk with balanced views*
- *Techniques for managing overthinking and confirmation bias*

CHAPTER 4: HIDDEN COSTS OF HOLDING ON TO REGRET

- *Physical and emotional toll of long-term regret*
- *How regret can erode confidence and relationships*
- *Identifying costs and learning to release them*

CHAPTER 5: DEALING WITH OVERWHELMING MEMORIES

- *Triggers that resurrect painful past events*
- *Calming methods to handle intense flashbacks*
- *Reframing memories to reduce their emotional impact*

CHAPTER 6: REDUCING SELF-BLAME AND ANGER

- Differences between healthy accountability and destructive guilt
- Approaches to tame anger directed inward and outward
- Practical steps for self-forgiveness

CHAPTER 7: RECOGNIZING WHAT YOU CANNOT CHANGE

- Identifying unchangeable facts and avoiding wasted effort
- Shifting focus from impossible fixes to constructive actions
- Using acceptance to channel energy toward the present

CHAPTER 8: METHODS TO SHIFT YOUR PERSPECTIVE

- Techniques to challenge negative assumptions
- Using humor, reframing, and mental distance
- Linking perspective change to improved emotional well-being

CHAPTER 9: PLANNING FOR FUTURE DECISIONS

- Strategies to reduce impulsive choices and risk of regret
- Setting clear goals and gathering reliable information
- Balancing logical thinking with emotional factors

CHAPTER 10: UNCOVERING PRACTICAL WAYS TO LEARN FROM REGRET

- Transforming regret into constructive lessons
- Spotting hidden patterns that repeat across regrets
- Turning insights into meaningful actions

CHAPTER 11: BUILDING STRONGER MENTAL HABITS

- Establishing daily thinking routines that prevent regrets
- Managing automatic thoughts and negativity
- Setting boundaries with yourself and your environment

TABLE OF CONTENTS

CHAPTER 1: UNDERSTANDING THE CONCEPT OF REGRET

- *How regret differs from guilt or shame*
- *Why regret can linger and affect daily life*
- *Initial strategies to shift from regret to insight*

CHAPTER 2: HOW REGRET DEVELOPS OVER TIME

- *Small decisions that grow into larger remorse*
- *Memory distortion and social influences on regret*
- *Practical ways to address regret early*

CHAPTER 3: THE INFLUENCE OF THOUGHT PATTERNS ON REGRET

- *Spotting negative filters and "if only" loops*
- *Replacing harmful self-talk with balanced views*
- *Techniques for managing overthinking and confirmation bias*

CHAPTER 4: HIDDEN COSTS OF HOLDING ON TO REGRET

- *Physical and emotional toll of long-term regret*
- *How regret can erode confidence and relationships*
- *Identifying costs and learning to release them*

CHAPTER 5: DEALING WITH OVERWHELMING MEMORIES

- *Triggers that resurrect painful past events*
- *Calming methods to handle intense flashbacks*
- *Reframing memories to reduce their emotional impact*

CHAPTER 6: REDUCING SELF-BLAME AND ANGER

- Differences between healthy accountability and destructive guilt
- Approaches to tame anger directed inward and outward
- Practical steps for self-forgiveness

CHAPTER 7: RECOGNIZING WHAT YOU CANNOT CHANGE

- Identifying unchangeable facts and avoiding wasted effort
- Shifting focus from impossible fixes to constructive actions
- Using acceptance to channel energy toward the present

CHAPTER 8: METHODS TO SHIFT YOUR PERSPECTIVE

- Techniques to challenge negative assumptions
- Using humor, reframing, and mental distance
- Linking perspective change to improved emotional well-being

CHAPTER 9: PLANNING FOR FUTURE DECISIONS

- Strategies to reduce impulsive choices and risk of regret
- Setting clear goals and gathering reliable information
- Balancing logical thinking with emotional factors

CHAPTER 10: UNCOVERING PRACTICAL WAYS TO LEARN FROM REGRET

- Transforming regret into constructive lessons
- Spotting hidden patterns that repeat across regrets
- Turning insights into meaningful actions

CHAPTER 11: BUILDING STRONGER MENTAL HABITS

- Establishing daily thinking routines that prevent regrets
- Managing automatic thoughts and negativity
- Setting boundaries with yourself and your environment

CHAPTER 12: STRATEGIES TO HANDLE EXTERNAL PRESSURES

- Societal, family, and workplace demands that spark regret
- Setting healthy boundaries and balancing competing needs
- Staying true to personal values despite outside influences

CHAPTER 13: IMPROVING EMOTIONAL SELF-CARE

- Recognizing and naming your emotions effectively
- Relaxation methods and healthy outlets for intense feelings
- Building a supportive environment that nurtures resilience

CHAPTER 14: TRANSFORMING REGRET INTO CONSTRUCTIVE INSIGHTS

- Using reflection and root-cause analysis to uncover lessons
- Applying insights in real-life scenarios
- Balancing emotional healing with pragmatic steps forward

CHAPTER 15: REPAIRING PERSONAL RELATIONSHIPS

- Apologizing genuinely and rebuilding trust
- Setting boundaries and learning from recurring conflicts
- Deciding when a relationship can be saved or must be released

CHAPTER 16: MANAGING LINGERING SHAME

- Differences between guilt and deep personal shame
- Shame's toxic cycle and ways to disrupt it
- Self-compassion as a stable antidote to self-criticism

CHAPTER 17: STRENGTHENING PROBLEM-SOLVING SKILLS

- Systems and frameworks for logical, calm decision-making
- Overcoming emotional blocks that lead to rushed choices
- Integrating problem-solving into daily routines

CHAPTER 18: MAINTAINING HOPE IN DAILY LIFE

- *Why hope is crucial for handling and avoiding regret*
- *Balancing realistic acceptance with a forward-looking mindset*
- *Habits and social connections that keep hope alive*

CHAPTER 19: SUSTAINING PROGRESS WITHOUT BACKSLIDING

- *Preventing old habits from resurfacing*
- *Creating supportive environments and accountability structures*
- *Tackling minor slips early before they grow into major setbacks*

CHAPTER 20: FINAL REFLECTIONS AND FUTURE OUTLOOK

- *Summarizing lessons from regret and integrating them into life*
- *Balancing accountability with kindness to oneself*
- *Creating a flexible, evolving plan that aligns with your deeper values*

CHAPTER 1: UNDERSTANDING THE CONCEPT OF REGRET

Regret is a complex reaction to actions or inaction in our past. Many people think regret is just about feeling sad for what has already happened, but it involves a range of thoughts and emotions. Some experience regret as a mild disappointment, while others feel a deep sense of loss that can color their entire worldview. It is not only about a bad choice; regret also surfaces when we believe we missed a better path. For instance, you might regret not learning a skill in your youth when you had more time. Or you might regret entering a relationship that caused emotional or financial harm. In any case, regret brings a mental burden that can last for days, months, or even years.

One way to better grasp regret is to look at how it affects our behavior. When you regret a past decision, you may feel tempted to reverse the outcome, if that were possible. Even though you know you cannot change the past, you might replay events in your mind, searching for small details that could have led you to a better choice. This process is called counterfactual thinking, a mental exercise where we imagine alternate scenarios. For example, a person who arrives too late for a flight might keep thinking, "If only I had left home ten minutes earlier." These mental pictures can help us learn from mistakes, but they can also lead to ongoing stress.

Regret can show itself in multiple ways. Some individuals withdraw from social activities or professional opportunities. They become fearful of making the same mistakes again. Others become overly cautious and hesitate at every decision point, unsure if their next choice will also lead to regret. Some attempt to run from regret by burying themselves in constant work or distractions. Although this strategy provides a short break from painful thoughts, it often does not resolve the deeper issues. The mind eventually goes back to the regretted event, sometimes with more intensity.

Modern psychology provides several explanations for regret. One concept is that regret is tied to our need for a sense of control. When we reflect on past mistakes, we try to figure out how to keep similar mistakes from happening again. By focusing on regret, we think we are solving a problem. However, this behavior can become excessive. It can transform into rumination, which is a repeated replay of negative thoughts with no clear solution. This kind of thinking only intensifies sadness or guilt.

To fully understand regret, it helps to compare it with related emotions like guilt and shame. Guilt often arises when we feel we have done something wrong. Regret, on the other hand, can happen even when no moral wrongdoing is involved. For instance, you might regret spending time on an unproductive hobby, even if no one was hurt by this choice. Shame is an emotion about who we are, rather than what we did. While regret focuses on a specific event or action, shame suggests a flaw in our character. In many cases, regret and shame overlap, causing a painful combination of self-blame and negative self-judgment.

When regret lasts too long, it can affect physical health. Stress hormones spike, blood pressure may rise, and the immune system can be impacted. Studies suggest that unrelenting regret might lead to higher risks of certain heart problems. This does not mean regret alone causes disease, but the combination of stress and despair from regret can wear down the body over time. People who get trapped in this emotional cycle often find it difficult to experience relief or rest. Their sleep might become disturbed, leaving them even more vulnerable to negative thinking.

One factor that shapes regret is our personal expectation of what "should" have happened. For instance, you might think that your career path "should" have been more impressive or more profitable. Or you might think you "should" have built a strong family by a certain age. When reality does not match these expectations, regret can take root. This gap between reality and expectation can feel like a personal failure, even when circumstances were out of your control.

Society also plays a role in how we form regret. Social media and popular culture often highlight success stories, fueling comparisons. When you see others who seem to have perfect achievements, you might conclude you made the wrong decisions. These comparisons can become a heavy load to carry because they make you feel that your position in life is far behind what it could have been. This leads to a sharper sense of regret. Such influences can distort our perception. You might forget that each person's path is different and that public images often mask hidden problems.

In many cultures, regret is sometimes seen as part of human life. People with a certain mindset feel that regret is useful for teaching caution. For example, regret can remind a person not to repeat reckless actions. However, the key is not to let that reminder turn into a lifetime prison. Balanced regret should lead to a plan to do better, not to endless self-condemnation. When regret remains balanced, it can serve as a helpful warning without blocking a person's development.

Researchers in behavioral economics have explored how regret influences decisions. They find that fear of regret can be more powerful than the wish for success. People will sometimes avoid action just because they do not want to feel regret later. This can lead to missed chances that could have been beneficial in the long term. For example, an individual might avoid investing money in a promising venture because they are terrified of regretting any potential loss. While caution is wise, an extreme reaction to the possibility of regret can limit overall progress.

The mind's design also shapes regret. Our brains are wired to notice and remember negative events more than positive ones. This means we tend to recall regrets clearly, sometimes revisiting them spontaneously when we see reminders or triggers. For instance, noticing an old photograph might bring back regrets about a lost friendship. This is linked to how the brain weighs negative experiences more heavily, likely for survival reasons. Our ancestors needed to remember what was dangerous or harmful to protect themselves. While that ability is useful for learning, it can also trap us in repeating regretful memories.

To break free from this mental trap, the first step is understanding what regret does to the mind. It can distract us, limit our self-confidence, and narrow our ability to plan ahead. It can also cause us to develop negative assumptions. For example, if you regret how you handled an important exam in college, you might start to think you are "terrible at taking tests" or "never able to make good decisions." These broad labels become part of your self-image, shaping how you see yourself in future tasks. Before long, you might lose motivation for any new challenge because you are convinced you will make poor choices again.

Another feature of regret is that it can linger, even when outcomes are generally positive. For example, imagine you did not take a certain job and went with a different path. Later, you may have a fine career, a decent income, and a satisfying daily life. Still, there can be a nagging voice in the back of your mind that wonders, "What if I had taken that other job?" This shows that regret sometimes does not depend on current hardships. Instead, it thrives on the unknown. We might fixate on the roads not taken, believing those other roads were better, even if the truth is uncertain. This mental pattern can cloud our appreciation of what we do have in the present.

In addition, regret can influence our willingness to trust ourselves. After a bad outcome, you might worry you are not reliable when it comes to making choices. This self-doubt can make you dependent on other people's opinions or overly reliant on external validation. You might look for constant reassurance that you are doing the right thing. Over time, this loss of self-trust can limit your freedom to grow. You may ask friends and family to weigh in on every matter because you fear making the "wrong" call. This can create tension in relationships, as others might feel pressured by your endless need for advice.

Understanding regret also means looking at how it can mask deeper problems. Sometimes, what we label as regret is actually frustration with our present conditions. We might say, "I regret not moving to a new city when I was younger," but the real issue could be dissatisfaction with our current social circle or lack of adventure in daily life. While regret pinpoints a past event, the deeper feeling might be a craving for excitement or a fear of stagnation. By sorting out these root problems, a person can better address regret and possibly reduce it by working on changes in current life circumstances.

Another layer of regret concerns how it interacts with envy or jealousy. You might regret not making certain moves in your career path if you see someone else who is now in a position you desire. The root of your regret might be envy, not just disappointment at your own action or inaction. This difference matters. If your main motivation is envy, you might not be addressing genuine regret. Instead, you are comparing yourself to others in a way that fosters self-criticism. Realizing this can free you from confusion and help you handle the emotion correctly.

It is also important to note the difference between regret for a specific choice and regret for not having enough information before making that choice. People often assume they should have known better, but in many cases, you simply did not have access to certain facts at the time. Realizing this can reduce the emotional pressure you place on yourself. For example, you might regret not buying a certain stock that later soared in value. But if you truly had no way of knowing it would rise, then your regret is not based on a fair view of the situation. Being honest about what you knew at the time can help you see that the outcome was out of your hands.

Society often glamorizes being fearless, praising those who say they have "no regrets." But this perspective overlooks the educational side of regret. Having no regrets might indicate that you have not reflected on your actions deeply enough, or it might be a defense mechanism to avoid unpleasant emotions. Healthy regret acknowledges we made certain choices that did not work out as intended, and we can use that realization to adjust our future steps.

In understanding regret, it is helpful to see that it has a function. In small doses, regret can be the mind's way of helping us learn from past errors. It can prompt us to set better boundaries, plan more carefully, or be more thoughtful in relationships. Regret only becomes a problem when it takes over our mental landscape. For some people, regret becomes so overwhelming that they cannot move forward. They remain stuck in the past, replaying the same script of "if only." They lose the ability to be fully present and to explore new possibilities.

An unusual but significant detail is that regret can be impacted by the time of day or even the seasons. Some individuals find that regretful thoughts peak at night, perhaps because there are fewer distractions. Others notice regret grows stronger in certain months, possibly tied to anniversaries of major events. Knowing these patterns is not common sense because many people do not track how regret changes with the calendar or daily schedule. By watching for these patterns, a person might figure out when to practice certain relaxation methods or avoid major decisions if regret is especially strong at those times.

In different age groups, regret can manifest differently. Younger individuals might regret not fitting in with their peers or missing out on certain social experiences. Those in middle age might regret missed career milestones or financial mistakes. Older adults might regret not spending enough time with loved ones or failing to follow personal dreams. Each stage of life comes with distinct focuses, and understanding this can help tailor the methods you use to manage regret. There is no one-size-fits-all plan for dealing with regret because the content of regret changes over time.

Part of understanding regret is recognizing that it can have a purpose if you choose to use it productively. For instance, a brief wave of regret after hurting a friend's feelings can lead you to apologize and restore the relationship. Without regret, you might not feel the need to correct your mistakes. But if regret continues and turns into self-punishment, it loses that beneficial quality. Understanding this balance is key for healthy emotional growth.

Finally, it is wise to remember that regret can sometimes be entangled with feelings of nostalgia. You may look at the past with a sense of romantic longing for how things used to be. This can blend with regret as you start to believe you should have acted differently to keep that old happiness alive. While nostalgia can remind you of good times, it can also enhance regret if you feel that you failed to protect a period of your life that seemed better than the present. Recognizing how nostalgia affects your understanding of the past is another step toward seeing regret clearly.

In sum, regret is not just a passing emotion. It is a multi-faceted response that includes reflection on past actions, possible alternate outcomes, moral judgments, and self-assessment. It can motivate positive change or trap us in a cycle of self-blame. By gaining a deeper view of how regret arises and influences our minds, we take the first step toward reducing its negative effects. The next chapters will build on this foundation by explaining how regret grows over time and how to keep it from taking control of our emotions and decisions.

CHAPTER 2: HOW REGRET DEVELOPS OVER TIME

Regret does not always appear right after a mistake or missed chance. Sometimes, it unfolds slowly, creeping into our thoughts and intensifying as we reflect on past events. This chapter explores how regret deepens over days, months, and even years, and shows that the passage of time can either help us make sense of regret or cause it to become more entrenched.

One hidden factor in the growth of regret is memory distortion. We do not always recall events precisely as they occurred. Our minds reconstruct past events each time we bring them to consciousness. This process can be tainted by our current mood, our self-esteem, or by new information we have gathered after the fact. For example, if you felt generally happy at the time of a certain decision, but now you are unhappy, you might adjust your memories to see that past decision as worse than it was. Alternatively, you might look back on an old romantic relationship and think it was perfect, overlooking real problems that were present. This altered memory can feed regret because it sets up a false comparison between a distorted past and the present reality.

A second factor is the social echo chamber. When people around you keep bringing up a past event, it can become fixed in your mind as something you should regret. Suppose you had the chance to study abroad but decided not to go due to family obligations. Over the years, friends or relatives might make remarks like, "You could be living a different life if you had gone." These repeated observations can solidify your regret, even if you had good reasons at the time. Social reinforcement of regret can be powerful, because it frames your past choice as an obvious error. Over time, you might question your own logic, concluding that you definitely missed a unique life path.

Technology adds another dimension to how regret grows. With social media, old memories are resurrected through "on this day" features or photo reminders. A post or picture from years ago can pop up, putting a spotlight on a decision you once made. This can catch you off guard and restart the cycle of regret. In the past, you would have had to flip through an old photo album to be reminded of a regret. Now these triggers appear automatically, with no warning. This constant flow of reminders can make regret develop more strongly than it would if certain events stayed in the background.

Another way regret develops is through the lens of new successes or failures. Imagine you make a decision about your career and later face obstacles or disappointments. During those difficult times, you might look back and think, "If I had done things differently, I would not be in this tough spot." Alternatively, if you see someone else succeed in a similar path you passed up, you might feel regret intensify. You compare your struggles to their achievements. This comparison amplifies regret, turning a once small pang of sorrow into a large source of sadness or resentment.

People also develop regret as they learn more about the consequences of their past actions. When we make decisions, we are guessing about the future based on what we know at the time. As months or years pass, new information comes to light that might paint the decision in a different color. For instance, you might discover that your choice to move to a certain city led you to miss out on a hidden job market somewhere else. Or you might learn that the degree you pursued is becoming obsolete in the modern workforce. As these facts accumulate, you might question your earlier conclusions and view them as naive or shortsighted. This expanded knowledge can make regret more acute, because you see that the cost of your old choice was higher than you initially believed.

In some cases, regret grows because people did not process the original disappointment at the time it happened. They may have brushed it aside or focused on other matters, thinking they could deal with it later. However, unprocessed emotion does not just disappear. It can resurface when triggered by new events that carry a similar theme. For example, if you regret how you handled a conflict with a sibling years ago, you might feel a surge of that old regret each time a new family issue arises. Over time, this pattern can expand the depth of regret. Each new conflict adds fuel to the old regret because you never settled your feelings about it in the first place.

Physical health problems or burnout can also worsen regret over time. When you are stressed or fatigued, your mind tends to focus on negative thoughts more than usual. During such times, unresolved regrets can emerge with greater force. Chronic pain or long-term illness, for instance, can lead you to rethink past decisions: "If I had taken better care of my body, maybe I would not be in this condition now." The physical discomfort amplifies mental distress, creating a vicious cycle. This link between body and mind is a key reason regret can intensify, rather than fade, as the years go by.

Another angle is how regret can become part of your identity. For instance, if you often speak about a certain regretful event, people might start identifying you with that narrative. They expect you to mention it whenever a related topic arises. Over time, you begin to see yourself primarily as "the person who messed up that one chance." It becomes a defining story for you. This identity-related regret does not just influence your thoughts, but also how others treat you. They might avoid inviting you to new opportunities, assuming you are still stuck on your old mistakes. This isolation can deepen regret because it confirms the idea that you are forever marked by your past choices.

The speed of life changes also affects regret. In modern times, job markets, social norms, and technology shift rapidly. A decision that seemed logical five years ago might now look like a missed opportunity due to how swiftly conditions changed. For instance, you might regret not learning a specific software skill when it was new, because now it is in high demand. As new success stories appear in the media, you might feel regret that you did not keep up with the changes. This sense of "falling behind" can grow more intense as time goes on, particularly if you sense that you are further and further away from what you imagine might have been a better path.

Moreover, regret can evolve when your core values shift. As people grow older or gain life experience, they sometimes adopt new principles or priorities. Something that did not seem essential in your twenties might become a primary focus in your forties. This change in perspective can transform a choice you once saw as harmless into a regretful event. For instance, you may not have valued family time strongly when you were younger, but now you might wish you had spent more time with relatives who have passed away. The sadness connected to this realization can expand over time, since you cannot go back and recapture those missed moments.

The emotional weight of regret is also shaped by how you process it. Some individuals repeatedly seek reassurance that they made the right choice, asking friends or colleagues to validate their decisions. When that reassurance is lacking or contradicts their expectations, regret grows stronger. This pattern of seeking external approval can become a crutch, preventing you from building an internal sense of certainty. Over time, if people around you become tired of comforting you, you might be left feeling more alone with your regret than ever. This can result in a self-perpetuating cycle: the more you seek validation, the less you get it, and the deeper your regret digs in.

Additionally, regret may gain momentum because we tend to compare ourselves to an idealized version of who we could have been. Psychologists sometimes call this "lost possible self." We imagine a parallel life where everything went perfectly, thinking that life would be free of regrets or challenges. This illusion can become more detailed over time as we keep adding what-ifs. Eventually, it seems like we missed the best path for ourselves, when in reality, that ideal version might have had its own set of problems. The problem is that we cannot compare real life to an imaginary scenario without ignoring many real-world complications.

Family history can also strengthen regret. If you come from a background where regret was treated as a sign of weakness, you might suppress it, causing it to fester and become more powerful in the subconscious. Or if your family passed down stories of "if only your grandfather had done this," you might inherit regrets that are not even your own. As the family narrative grows, these regrets can shape your life choices. You might feel compelled to fix what older relatives regretted, or you might blame yourself for continuing a pattern of regret. With time, these inherited regrets mingle with your personal regrets, forming a layered sense of disappointment that is harder to unravel.

Interestingly, regret can become more apparent when you achieve a significant victory in life. A promotion, a big award, or a major personal milestone might trigger thoughts of "I wish I had gotten this sooner" or "If I had done X differently, I would have reached this level a long time ago." This ironic effect happens because successes can highlight how far you might have come if not for past mistakes. Instead of simply enjoying the new achievement, you might end up reflecting on what could have been. Over time, each success can remind you of the path not taken, reinforcing regret rather than relieving it.

Another subtle factor in the evolution of regret is the influence of cultural norms. In some settings, people are told to stay positive and never speak of mistakes. This can discourage open expression of regret, leading it to turn into silent shame. Over time, unspoken regret festers, taking root in the subconscious. In environments where talking about regret is seen as healthy, people might be able to process it sooner and prevent it from growing into a life-blocking emotional burden. Thus, the culture you live in can shape whether your regrets get smaller or larger as time passes.

Finally, regret can develop in layers. You might first regret a specific decision, such as dropping out of a training program. Later, you might regret how you responded to that regret—perhaps you lashed out at others or avoided new opportunities because you were ashamed. Over months or years, a chain reaction can occur: you regret the original act, then you regret your response to that regret, and so forth. Each stage adds new depth to the emotional load.

These various influences show how regret is not a simple feeling that appears once and then leaves. It can shift, grow, or fade over a period, depending on how we handle it and what new events arise. The slow accumulation of regret is often what causes people to feel they have missed out on large parts of life. However, the fact that regret develops gradually also provides chances to confront it at different points. If we remain aware of how regret evolves, we can step in before it becomes too big to handle.

Chapter 2 reveals that regret is more than a single flash of sorrow. It is a process that can be shaped by social factors, memory biases, new information, and shifting personal values. Keeping track of these influences can reduce the power regret has over your life. In the next chapters, we will discuss how certain thought patterns feed regret and learn about methods to disrupt these patterns before they lead to long-term distress. By seeing regret as a dynamic process rather than an unchangeable fact, we can begin to loosen its grip and move toward a healthier view of both past and future.

CHAPTER 3: THE INFLUENCE OF THOUGHT PATTERNS ON REGRET

Regret often grows when we fall into specific ways of thinking. These patterns can intensify our negative feelings and make it harder to move past old mistakes or missed chances. While it is natural to reflect on what we could have done differently, certain habits of thought transform those reflections into a more destructive mindset. In this chapter, we look at how common thought patterns stir up regret, how our mental processes can lock us into a cycle of sorrow, and what uncommon strategies might help us avoid getting stuck.

The Role of Negative Filters

One major factor that shapes regret is the habit of using negative filters. This occurs when we focus on the worst side of a situation or mentally spotlight anything that went wrong, while ignoring everything that went right. Suppose you applied for a new job and reached the final round of interviews but did not get hired. If you only focus on the rejection, you might feel a sharp regret that you "failed" or "wasted your time." However, this outlook ignores the good steps you took in gaining interview experience or building connections. Over time, negative filters can lead you to think that every important event ends in regret, reinforcing an unhelpful mindset that overlooks progress and growth.

A lesser-known approach to tackling negative filters is to document the positive outcomes that still happened despite an unwelcome result. For example, listing three ways the event contributed to your development—even if it ended in a letdown—can reduce the strength of regret. This practice might seem simple, but many people do not do it because they assume it will not help. In reality, shifting your focus to include positive elements can neutralize the mental process that exaggerates the negative. By keeping a record of these overlooked positives, you train your mind to look for them more automatically, lowering the chance that regret will take over.

Catastrophic Thinking and Regret

Catastrophic thinking is another pattern that intensifies regret. This involves imagining the worst possible future outcome based on a past mistake. For instance, if you regret mishandling your finances last year, you might start thinking you will never recover financially, that you will end up in debt forever, or that you have ruined your life beyond repair. While it is good to be realistic about the impact of errors, viewing them as permanent disasters can block you from seeing possible solutions.

One unusual but effective strategy against catastrophic thinking is to play out a fair-minded scenario side by side with the worst-case one. For example, if you are convinced that a financial mistake dooms your future, set aside time to list clear facts about your current resources, your ability to earn money, and the help you can get. This balanced approach challenges the assumption that a single mistake dictates the rest of your life. It may not completely remove your regret, but it can bring your attention to actual possibilities rather than imagined horrors.

"If Only" Loops

Many people with chronic regret get stuck in "if only" loops. These loops are a cycle of thoughts where you keep telling yourself things like, "If only I had studied harder," "If only I had asked for advice," or "If only I had taken that other path." On the surface, such thoughts may seem like ordinary wishes for a better outcome. But they become a problem when they replay endlessly, blocking progress.

A direct method to handle "if only" loops is to convert each of these statements into a concrete lesson. Instead of just saying, "If only I had studied harder," translate that into, "I can plan a stricter study schedule in the future." This small shift changes a backward-looking complaint into a forward-looking plan. By assigning an actionable step to each "if only," you reduce the mental hold of regret because your mind gains a practical assignment instead of an open-ended lament.

Perfectionism and Its Link to Regret

Perfectionism is a significant contributor to regret because it sets unrealistic standards for success or behavior. When we do not meet these high expectations, regret spikes. A person who aims for perfection in everything may look back at a past event and see any small flaw as a glaring failure. This makes it easy to regret not having been "perfect." People sometimes claim perfectionism is a good trait because it pushes them to excel. However, persistent perfectionism can become harmful when it turns every shortcoming into a source of deep regret.

A lesser-known remedy for perfectionism is to engage in deliberate "allowable mistakes." This means picking low-stake activities—like learning a hobby—and setting a target to be just "sufficient" instead of perfect. During this process, you might allow yourself to do a sloppy job on one or two tasks, with the intention of observing your emotional reaction. This exercise helps you see that the world does not collapse when you perform at a level below your perfect standard. Over time, you can apply this mindset to more areas, reducing the intensity of regret that comes from failing to achieve impossible goals.

Mental Comparisons and Regret

Comparing our lives to others is a major culprit in building regret. Social media and casual conversation often center on achievements, which can lead us to think we are behind in every way. For instance, if you see a peer who became a parent early or who started a profitable business, you might regret your choices because you feel you missed what they have. But these comparisons do not include the entire story of the other person's hardships, trade-offs, or private fears.

An uncommon but helpful way to handle these comparisons is to keep a "personal progress log." Instead of measuring your life against someone else, measure your current state against where you were six months or a year ago. Did you gain any new skill? Did you improve your social circle, even slightly? By focusing on your own track record, you direct attention toward self-improvement and away from external yardsticks. This shift can reduce regret because it pulls your mind away from unrealistic or unfair comparisons.

Self-Talk That Shapes Regret

Another layer of thought patterns has to do with how we speak to ourselves internally. Many people use harsh language when they think about their errors. For example, they might say, "I was stupid to do that," or "I always mess things up." This constant self-criticism sets a tone that amplifies regret. If you label yourself as someone who is always failing, regret becomes your default response to mistakes. It becomes harder to see missteps as isolated incidents rather than as evidence of a flawed identity.

A practical method to adjust harmful self-talk is to replace absolute statements with specific, limited ones. Instead of saying, "I always mess up," say, "I messed up this one time." Such small changes in wording can lead to big shifts in emotion. Over time, this simple strategy can help you stop painting your entire self with a negative brush. By not using rigid labels for yourself, you leave room for improvement and you shrink the scope of regret.

Overthinking and Confirmation Bias

Overthinking is a pattern where we analyze every detail of a past mistake, hoping to find an explanation that will bring peace. But excessive analysis can trap us in a cycle of self-blame, particularly when combined with confirmation bias. Confirmation bias is our tendency to interpret new information in a way that agrees with our existing views. If you already believe you made a terrible choice, you will latch onto any detail that supports that belief, ignoring facts that might show otherwise.

One unusual approach to reducing overthinking is to schedule a "rumination window." You might say, "I will allow myself 15 minutes after dinner to think about this regret." Outside of that window, if you catch your thoughts spinning, you remind yourself, "I will deal with this during my set time." This method works against overthinking by containing it, rather than letting it spread throughout the day. Eventually, you might find you have fewer regrets or see them in a smaller light because they are not constantly hijacking your thoughts.

Sunk Cost Fallacy and Regret

The sunk cost fallacy is when we continue with an action just because we have already invested time or resources in it, even if it is no longer beneficial. People who realize they have fallen into this trap often feel regret for not cutting their losses earlier. For instance, someone might stay in a project for years, draining money and energy, before finally quitting. Once they exit, they might feel regret for all that wasted effort.

To avoid regret linked to sunk costs, a helpful strategy is a regular review of ongoing commitments. Every quarter or so, list your major commitments—jobs, relationships, side projects—and rate each one's current value to your life goals. If it is no longer helping you, consider reducing or ending it without feeling like the past investment must dictate your future. This is not common sense to everyone because we are often taught to stay loyal to our initial choices. But letting go at the right time can prevent deeper regret in the long run.

Groupthink and Regret

Sometimes, regret arises when we follow a group decision rather than our own judgment. After a bad group outcome, individuals might look back and think, "I knew it would end badly. Why didn't I say something?" This leads to regret for not standing up for what we believed. Groupthink occurs when members of a group avoid conflict and go along with the majority to keep harmony, even if they privately disagree.

One approach to limit groupthink-based regret is to rotate the role of "devil's advocate" in group discussions. Each time you meet, assign one person to question the consensus actively, even if they personally agree with it. This lowers the pressure to conform and can reveal flaws in the plan. It also helps everyone voice their concerns before the decision is made. If the final choice still goes wrong, you may experience less regret because you had a fair process that allowed for dissent.

Automatic Thoughts and Mindfulness

Research suggests that many of our thoughts occur in an automatic mode, shaped by habits and emotions we are not aware of. These automatic thoughts can repeatedly highlight our regrets without our conscious choice. We might suddenly recall a past failure when we see a random sign or hear a familiar song. This triggers feelings of sadness or anger, reinforcing the cycle of regret.

A lesser-known tool to manage automatic thoughts is to label them quickly without judgment. For instance, when a regretful memory floats up, you could mentally say, "That is a regret thought," then gently switch your focus to a neutral subject, like counting your breaths or noticing nearby sounds. This labeling practice is rooted in a simple form of mindfulness training but does not require deep meditation sessions. By labeling the thought and moving on, you break the automatic link between a reminder and the flood of negative feelings.

The Expectation Gap

Thought patterns tied to expectations can also fuel regret. If we set our sights on a certain outcome and reality falls short, regret is a frequent result. This expectation gap can be internal—such as believing we should be at a specific point in our career by a certain age—or external, such as believing family members should behave in a particular way. When the real world does not match these expectations, disappointment and regret follow.

To reduce regret from the expectation gap, conduct a regular "expectation audit." Write down your top expectations and assess which ones are truly within your control. If you discover that some expectations rely on factors outside your influence, you can adjust them. This might mean changing your timeline or redefining what success looks like. This practice prevents you from setting yourself up for regret by tying your sense of worth to events that you cannot command.

The Inner Critic and Regret

Most people have an inner critic, a mental voice that scolds us for not being good enough. This inner critic might say, "You did that wrong again," or "You're hopeless." It is a major factor in fueling regret because it frames everything in a negative way. When you look back on a decision, the inner critic quickly judges you as incompetent or lazy, ignoring context or complexity. Over time, this can create a loop where regret feeds the inner critic, and the critic inflames regret.

To tackle the inner critic, one rare but effective technique is to assign it a separate persona in your mind. Give it a name or imagine it as a cartoon character. Then, when it starts its harsh commentary, you can address it from a distance, like, "I hear you, but I don't need your input right now." This approach may sound odd, but it helps you see the critic as just one element of your thoughts rather than an ultimate source of truth. Over time, this separation can reduce the critic's power to magnify regret.

Unhelpful Mentors and Regret

Often, we do not think about how advice from others can plant seeds of regret. Sometimes, mentors—whether they are friends, family, or professionals—can impose their own values or ideals on us. If we follow advice that goes against our own intuition and end up with bad results, we feel regret. Later, we might say, "I wish I had trusted my own instincts instead of listening to them." This form of regret is tied to letting others shape our choices.

To handle this, maintain an "advice log." Note down what key people recommend and see if their advice conflicts with your personal values or facts you know. This might seem tedious, but it can help you spot patterns. If a particular individual often pushes you in directions that lead to regret, it may be time to reduce their influence on your decisions. This process is not about ignoring good counsel, but about learning to weigh outside input against your own sense of direction.

Reducing the Power of Memory Triggers

Memory triggers can spring up from everyday items like a piece of clothing, a social media post, or a location you once visited. These triggers can send you back into a strong state of regret, even if you thought you had moved on. Over time, repeated exposure to triggers can strengthen the link between them and feelings of regret, making it very hard to break the cycle.

An uncommon way to weaken these triggers is to reframe their meaning. Let's say you have a souvenir from a trip that ended with deep regret. Instead of hiding the souvenir, you could rename it a "lesson reminder" in your mind. Each time you see it, you consciously tell yourself: "This item reminds me to act differently in the future." You convert the trigger from a sign of regret into a sign of growth. This re-labeling does not erase the past, but it helps shift your emotional reaction so that regret does not dominate.

Overreliance on Hindsight

A significant mental habit that inflames regret is thinking we "should have known better" when we made a decision in the past. This is a type of hindsight bias where we judge ourselves as if we had all the information at that time. The reality is, many decisions involve uncertainty. If you had known the outcome would be negative, you would not have chosen that path. Recognizing the role of unknown factors can help reduce the sense of self-blame that shapes regret.

A practical solution is to systematically document why you made a key decision when you made it. Write down the information you had, the pros and cons, and the risks you were aware of. Then, if regret surfaces later, you can look back at these notes. This direct evidence reminds you that you made the choice based on limited data, and hindsight was not available. It can be a potent counterbalance to the false assumption that you should have predicted the future accurately.

Emotional Reasoning

Emotional reasoning means letting your current feelings define how you judge past events. If you are sad today because of unrelated stress, you might color past decisions as worse than they were. Regret thrives on this emotional distortion because it adds more negative weight to an old memory. If you are angry at yourself for some current mistake, you may extend that anger to older decisions as well, creating a chain of self-criticism.

A lesser-known tactic to disrupt emotional reasoning is to place a mental "checkpoint" in each day. For example, at lunchtime, you might pause and quickly label your mood on a 1-to-10 scale (1 being very negative, 10 being very positive). If you notice you are at a low number, you can remind yourself that any regretful memories you recall during this time may be enlarged by your mood. This checkpoint fosters awareness of how your present emotional state may be warping your sense of the past.

Closing Thoughts on Thought Patterns

All of these mental tendencies—negative filters, catastrophic thinking, "if only" loops, perfectionism, comparisons, harsh self-talk, overthinking, confirmation bias, the sunk cost fallacy, groupthink, automatic negative thoughts, the expectation gap, the inner critic, influences from misguided mentors, memory triggers, hindsight bias, and emotional reasoning—merge in complex ways. Each can amplify regret if left unchecked. However, by noticing and adjusting these patterns, you can significantly weaken regret's grip.

It is not about forcing yourself to never recall mistakes or ignoring lessons from the past. Instead, it is about guiding your thoughts so they do not repeatedly push you into the same pit of sadness. By applying the less common techniques—like scheduling a rumination window, keeping an advice log, creating a personal progress record, reframing triggers, or naming the inner critic—you equip your mind with fresh tools. These strategies are not obvious and may require some effort to maintain, but they can break the long-standing habits that fuel regret.

In the next chapter, we will explore the hidden costs of holding on to regret. While many people recognize that regret is unpleasant, they may not realize how it quietly affects different areas of life, including personal relationships, health, and professional success. By identifying these hidden costs, you can gain extra motivation to use the thought-pattern strategies from this chapter and begin freeing yourself from the emotional weight of regret.

CHAPTER 4: HIDDEN COSTS OF HOLDING ON TO REGRET

Regret is often described as a heavy feeling in the heart or an anxious sense of missed chances. Yet, its influence can stretch much further than simple emotional discomfort. Holding on to regret can affect your relationships, health, sense of purpose, and overall progress. This chapter takes a close look at the costs of regret that are less obvious but can be very harmful. It also explains how these costs might build up silently and how to spot them before they create deeper troubles.

Strained Relationships

One major hidden cost of regret is the strain it places on personal bonds. When you hold on to regret, you might become distant with friends or family members who remind you of your past decisions. For example, if you regret not pursuing a certain career path, you might avoid relatives who work in that field, as their success highlights your regret. Over time, this can weaken important connections.

Regret can also lead to clingy behavior in relationships, especially if you regret letting someone important go in the past. You may fear repeating that mistake, so you hold on too tightly to new friends or romantic partners. This can create tension because the other person might feel smothered or responsible for your emotional needs. The irony is that by trying not to lose someone again, you might push them away. Recognizing this tendency early can spare both you and the other person unnecessary stress.

An unusual approach to addressing regret's impact on relationships is to create specific discussion boundaries. Inform your loved ones that you acknowledge your regret, but you are also working to change it. Ask them not to bring it up casually, and assure them you will do the same. This keeps regret from dominating every conversation, allowing relationships to exist outside the shadow of past mistakes. By setting these boundaries, you ensure that your bonds are built on current interactions, not defined by old regrets.

Eroded Self-Confidence

When regret becomes a continuous background noise, it can erode your self-confidence. Each time you recall a mistake, you might question your judgment or doubt your ability to make good choices. Over time, this self-doubt can take root, influencing every decision. A person who carries persistent regret may not apply for promotions, may avoid learning new skills, or even refuse social invitations because of fear of further mistakes.

This lack of confidence can lead to a vicious cycle: the more you avoid challenges, the less you gain from new experiences. That, in turn, can deepen regret because you miss chances for personal or professional growth. This cycle can continue for years if unchecked, depriving you of achievements that would have boosted your self-esteem.

To break this pattern, it can help to establish what some psychologists call "small wins." Pick tasks that are just beyond your comfort zone but still achievable. Successfully completing these tasks signals to your mind that your past mistakes do not define you. Although many have heard the idea of building self-confidence through small goals, they often do not link it directly to regret. Seeing how small successes can chip away at regret is not common sense, but it can be a powerful method to restore faith in your abilities.

Physical Health Consequences

Not everyone realizes that regret has physical effects. Long-term stress from regret can lead to elevated cortisol levels, which in turn might affect blood pressure, sleep quality, and even the immune system. Some studies suggest that unrelieved regret can contribute to chronic conditions, although it is rarely the sole cause. The body and mind are deeply connected, and negative emotions like regret can disrupt normal biological functions if they persist without relief.

Another hidden aspect is how regret can lead to unhealthy coping behaviors. Some people might adopt poor eating habits, substance use, or other harmful actions to distract themselves from regret. These choices may offer a short break from emotional pain, but they often create new problems that compound the original regret. In the long run, such habits not only harm physical health but also add to mental burdens, because the person then regrets these new behaviors as well.

A unique but practical solution is to set up periodic health check-ins tied to your emotional state. For instance, each month you might measure your stress levels in a simple notebook and note any physical symptoms (headaches, stomach issues, fatigue). If you see a pattern where these symptoms worsen when regret is prominent, it is a clear sign that holding on to regret is draining your health. Recognizing this correlation can motivate you to seek better coping tools.

Loss of Future Opportunities

When people remain stuck in regret, they often miss out on promising opportunities. One reason is that regret can sap mental energy, leaving you fatigued or preoccupied. Another is that regret might make you fearful of repeating mistakes, so you pass on new chances that carry any risk. Over time, these missed opportunities accumulate into further regret, creating a feedback loop. You regret the past, which causes you to shrink from the future, which leads to more regret.

One unusual way to counter this is to keep a "risk and gain" tracker. Each week, force yourself to take one new small risk—something as simple as chatting with a stranger at a social event or volunteering for a minor project at work. In the tracker, list what you gained by taking that risk, even if the outcome was not perfect. This ongoing record helps you realize that small risks usually do not end in terrible regrets. Rather, they can open doors or build new connections, chipping away at the fear-based mindset that feeds regret.

Worsening of Decision-Making Skills

Regret can distort how we make choices because we might over-correct to avoid the same misstep. For example, if you regret rushing into a business venture, you might later become too slow and miss windows of opportunity. Alternatively, if you regret not taking a big leap in the past, you might later jump into situations without enough planning, just to avoid feeling that old regret again. Both extremes show how regret can hamper balanced thinking.

Moreover, when regret dominates our thoughts, it can be harder to analyze present-day facts and probabilities. Instead, we focus on the emotional memory of the past. This leads us to rely on gut reactions influenced by fear or shame rather than solid reasoning. Over time, these fear-driven or shame-driven decisions can multiply, producing yet more regrets.

A method to handle this distortion is to use structured decision-making. For big decisions, lay out a simple table with the pros, cons, risks, and potential benefits. Then, note how much your regret from the past is pushing you toward or away from each choice. Seeing this on paper helps you detect if you are leaning too heavily on regret-based fear. That awareness can bring a more balanced perspective and keep old regrets from clouding your judgment.

Stunted Emotional Growth

Regret tends to keep emotional wounds fresh, preventing a person from learning lessons in a healthy manner. When regret is left unexamined, it blocks the normal process of emotional growth. You might remain stuck in an old emotional state, unable to progress to acceptance or resolution. This stunted growth can manifest as irritability, mood swings, or a sense that you are not the same person you were before the regret set in.

This hidden cost affects how you perceive new challenges and relationships. If your emotional growth is halted, you may lack the maturity to handle conflicts, speak calmly about your needs, or empathize with others. This can reduce your quality of life, making everyday experiences feel heavier than they are.

One rare but effective tactic to spark emotional growth is creative self-expression with a specific intention. For example, you might record short audio notes where you talk about your regret and then respond to yourself as if you were comforting a friend. This process can feel awkward, but it can unlock a more nurturing part of your mind. Unlike traditional journaling, this exercise involves hearing your tone of voice, which can reveal emotions you might not notice in silent writing. Over time, this helps you move past the point of emotional stagnation.

Social Isolation

Regret can encourage patterns of withdrawal from social settings. You might feel unworthy of friendship or think others view you negatively because of your past mistakes. This can lead you to skip gatherings, avoid phone calls, and quietly drift away from supportive networks. The real cost is a shrinking social circle that leaves you more vulnerable to negative thoughts.

Additionally, social isolation can create new regrets. You may later feel sorry that you did not maintain certain friendships or participate in group events when you had the chance. This is how regret can spawn more regret, leading to a long chain of sorrow. In some cases, people even lose the ability to enjoy positive social experiences because they have built a habit of pulling away.

To counter social withdrawal, try setting a small target for weekly social interactions, such as meeting a friend for coffee or attending a local community event. Afterward, note any positive outcomes, even if they seem minor. This ongoing record serves as a reminder that social interactions can be a net gain. It helps fight the internal script that says, "There is no point in going out; I will only feel more regret."

Effects on Creativity and Innovation

When weighed down by regret, creative thinking and innovation can suffer. The mind becomes consumed with replaying old scenarios rather than exploring new possibilities. If you work in a field that requires fresh ideas or inventive approaches, regret can dull your imaginative capacity. You might stick to safe methods, fearing that creativity will lead to mistakes and hence more regret.

One way to protect your creativity is to set aside "experiment time." During this period—maybe once a week—you give yourself permission to try something completely new without worrying about outcomes. This could be brainstorming a new business concept, experimenting with an art technique, or taking a different approach to problem-solving. By labeling it as "experiment time," you remind yourself that this space is free from the usual regret calculations. This can help you maintain or even boost creativity despite regrets that exist in other areas of your life.

Financial Ramifications

Regret can indirectly influence your finances as well. If you feel you have made one big money error, you might become so risk-averse that you never invest or explore better career paths. Or you might swing in the other direction, making impulsive decisions to overcompensate for past caution. Both scenarios can result in ongoing money troubles that add new layers of regret.

Financial counselors sometimes see clients who are not purely irrational with money but are weighed down by deep regret from earlier financial setbacks. Their self-image as "bad with money" keeps them from learning more about budgeting or investing. This self-fulfilling idea then ensures they continue to make poor financial choices. The hidden cost is that they remain in a loop of monetary stress, never escaping the regret that started it all.

A less obvious solution is to find a "financial buddy," someone you can check in with regularly about budgeting, saving, or investing. This should be a person you trust, but not someone who will shame you for past errors. By making finances a shared conversation rather than a lonely regret, you reduce the stress and open the door to consistent improvement. Over time, better financial habits can weaken the regrets tied to money mistakes.

Missed Chances for Leadership

If regret undermines your confidence and clarity, you might miss chances to be a leader in your workplace or community. Holding on to regret can cause you to second-guess yourself to the point where you do not volunteer for leadership roles, speak up in meetings, or offer bold ideas. This creates a hidden cost: you forfeit the growth that comes from leading, along with the benefits of recognition and career advancement.

Some people do not link leadership opportunities with regret, but the connection is strong. Fear of potential failure, stoked by old regrets, prevents them from taking steps that could strengthen their leadership abilities. If you never practice leading, you might regret your lost potential in the future. This is how regret can ripple across time, blocking you from achievements you might have handled successfully.

To break this pattern, consider starting small in leadership-like tasks. That might mean organizing a volunteer event with a few people or heading a short-term group project. Doing well in these smaller settings can weaken old regrets that say, "You are not capable," and start laying a foundation for bigger leadership roles later.

Limited Personal Identity

Regret can narrow how you see yourself. Instead of having a broad identity built on multiple interests, experiences, and talents, you might reduce yourself to "the person who messed up that one big thing." Over time, this limited identity becomes a self-fulfilling cycle, as you do not invest in other parts of your life. You might stop exploring new hobbies or professional paths because you feel your identity is already defined by regret.

A rare but effective remedy is to plan "identity expansion" activities. This means dedicating time to pursuits that have no direct connection to your source of regret. If your regret is career-related, do something unrelated, like volunteering at an animal shelter or learning a new language. The point is to gather experiences that broaden your sense of self. This approach goes beyond typical self-improvement because it specifically tackles the identity freeze that often comes with holding on to regret.

Emotional Exhaustion

Carrying regret can lead to constant mental fatigue, which is different from the usual tiredness you feel after a busy day. Emotional exhaustion occurs when your mental resources are used up by persistent worry, self-criticism, and negative reflection. Over weeks or months, this can develop into burnout, affecting your ability to be present in daily life.

People dealing with emotional exhaustion might also struggle with concentration, making it tough to complete tasks at work or school. This again can lead to more regret as they miss deadlines or deliver subpar results. It becomes a loop: regret leads to exhaustion, which leads to poor performance, which leads to fresh regret.

A strategy to manage emotional exhaustion involves "micro-rest" sessions. For instance, schedule a 5-minute break every two hours where you do something that calms your mind—like humming a tune, walking around the block, or looking at pictures of nature. This might not sound revolutionary, but it is not common sense for everyone to break the cycle of regret-fueled exhaustion in such small intervals. Over time, these micro-rests can rebuild your mental reserves, leaving less space for regret to erode your energy.

Ethical and Moral Dimensions

Regret can sometimes cloud moral judgment. You may focus so heavily on your old mistakes that you overlook present ethical responsibilities. For instance, you may feel you have already "failed" morally or ethically in one area, so why try to uphold good standards now? This sense of moral defeat can dull your sense of right and wrong in future actions. Alternatively, you might become overly strict with yourself and others, seeking moral purity to erase your past regrets.

Either extreme can harm your moral balance. A neglected angle is that regret might make you more self-focused, so you pay less attention to the needs of others. Locked in self-blame, you fail to notice someone else's troubles. This can erode your empathy and your positive influence on the people around you.

To keep a healthy moral perspective, set aside a short time each week to think about how you can help others. This might be a small act of kindness or volunteering for a local cause. By purposely shifting your focus to positive moral actions, you remind yourself that regret does not define your entire moral character. You still have the power to do good and make fresh ethical decisions.

Impact on Legacy

Legacy is what you leave behind—your contributions, relationships, and the memories people have of you. Holding on to regret can interfere with building a meaningful legacy. If you are always fixated on old regrets, you might not invest in mentoring younger people, creating community projects, or preserving family history. You might think you have nothing of value to pass on because you failed in the past.

This is a hidden cost because it only becomes clear when it is almost too late to do much about it. A person near the end of their career or life might look back and realize that regret stopped them from leaving a positive mark on others. By recognizing the danger early, you can take steps to shape the story you leave behind. Something as small as writing down family recipes or teaching a skill to a neighbor can reclaim a sense of contribution that regret threatens to steal.

Conclusion on Hidden Costs

Regret can silently infiltrate many parts of life—your health, your finances, your relationships, and your sense of identity. The costs go beyond moments of sadness or guilt. They include missed opportunities, stunted emotional growth, social isolation, creative blockages, and even moral and ethical confusion. Being aware of these hidden costs can serve as motivation to address regret more actively rather than letting it fester in the background.

As we continue through this book, the following chapters will cover methods to reduce these costs by managing overwhelming memories, reducing self-blame, and reorienting your thought patterns. By recognizing how deeply regret can affect you, you can take decisive steps to lighten its load. The good news is that many of these hidden costs can be reversed or lessened once you begin to release regret or transform it into constructive lessons.

CHAPTER 5: DEALING WITH OVERWHELMING MEMORIES

Regret can feel strongest when specific memories come back with force. These memories can appear when triggered by certain sights, sounds, places, or even random thoughts. At times, they can be so powerful that you feel transported back to the moment of your regret, reliving the disappointment or remorse. This chapter explains how overwhelming memories work, how they become linked to regret, and what methods can reduce their power.

Why Some Memories Are Overwhelming

Not all past events trigger strong regret. Often, the difference comes from the emotional significance attached to a memory. If a decision or mistake caused major pain, embarrassment, or loss, your brain stores those details with high priority. This can lead to strong recall later. Memories tied to significant emotions, such as guilt, heartbreak, or shock, might be easier for your mind to reactivate.

An uncommon insight is that your brain sometimes "reinforces" these memories each time you recall them. Neuroscientists refer to a process called memory reconsolidation. When you remember a past event, you briefly make it "flexible," meaning it can be altered slightly before it's stored again. If you focus on the regretful or painful side each time, you reinforce those negative feelings. But if you change how you interpret the memory (for instance, by adding new insights about what you learned or how it led to a different outcome later), you can gradually reshape the emotional load connected to that memory.

Recognizing Triggers

Overwhelming memories typically appear in response to triggers. A trigger might be a piece of music that you listened to during a difficult time, a location where something regretful happened, or a photo that stirs up old feelings. Triggers can also be internal, like a fleeting mood or an unrelated thought that somehow reminds you of the event. When a memory is closely linked to regret, these triggers can unleash intense reactions before you even realize what's going on.

Many people try to avoid triggers altogether. However, total avoidance can limit your life, especially if the triggers are common or tied to everyday situations. For example, if you regret a past relationship, you might try to steer clear of all reminders, such as certain restaurants or mutual friends. This approach can shrink your social world. The trick is not to eliminate every reminder but to change the way you respond to them.

Methods to Soften the Shock of Memories

1. **Gradual Exposure With a Goal**: Instead of full avoidance, consider planned, gentle exposure to a small piece of the trigger. If a particular photograph causes you distress, start by looking at it for a short time while focusing on calm breathing. The key difference is that you enter the situation with an intention: "I'm going to look at this photo for 30 seconds and remind myself that I can handle the feelings." This structured approach breaks the pattern of sudden, uncontrolled exposure, making the memory less overpowering in the long run.
2. **Mental Reframing**: Each time you recall the regretful moment, try adding a fresh perspective. For instance, if you regret dropping out of a training program, think about any positive changes that happened afterward, even if they seemed minor at the time. Maybe leaving that program gave you a chance to explore new interests or meet new people who shaped your life in another way. By folding these alternative insights into the memory, you disrupt its purely negative form.
3. **Concrete Anchors**: This strategy involves grounding techniques that anchor you in the present moment. When an overwhelming memory appears, quickly shift your focus to something in your current environment—like describing a physical object or naming five objects you see around you. This approach might sound simple, but it is effective because it calms the stress response, reminding the brain that you're in a different setting now.
4. **Body-Based Calming**: Strong memories can produce a surge of physical symptoms: racing heartbeat, tense muscles, or shallow breathing. Using body-based methods—like progressive muscle relaxation, slow breathing exercises, or massaging your hands—can lower the intensity of these symptoms. Once the body calms down, the mental grip of the memory often weakens as well.

Rethinking the Narrative

Sometimes, overwhelming memories owe their strength to the story we tell ourselves about what happened. If the internal narrative is "That day ruined my life," each recall of the memory reinforces the sense of total ruin. But if we adjust the story to "That day was a major setback, but it pushed me to make different choices," we reduce the memory's harmful impact. This is not about lying to ourselves; it's about highlighting facts we might have ignored.

A helpful practice here is writing a "then vs. now" comparison. On one side, list how you felt when the regretful event happened, what you believed about the situation, and how you saw yourself. On the other side, describe your current situation, your present beliefs, and any strengths you've built. This exercise shows that you have changed since then, which can lessen the feeling of being locked into the same painful context. When you see evidence of growth, the memory loses its power to define you.

Handling Intrusive Imagery

Some memories come as vivid mental pictures, replaying the moment of regret. You might see the exact scene: faces of people involved, items in the room, or precise details of the environment. These images can be startling and lead to spirals of sadness or anxiety.

An unusual technique to handle intrusive imagery is to alter small details in the mental replay. For example, if you always picture yourself wearing a certain outfit in that memory, imagine changing it to something else. Or change the color of the walls in the remembered space. This might sound trivial, but it disrupts the automated replay and helps your brain recognize that the memory is something it can reshape. By tinkering with details, you loosen the hold of the original emotional script.

Emotional Temperature Checks

When a memory is overwhelming, it can flood you with strong emotions such as shame or fear. One method to tackle this is to do "emotional temperature checks." Rate how strong your regret or anxiety is on a scale of 1 to 10 at different times: before, during, and after recalling the memory. This helps you see that your distress level can rise and fall, rather than stay at a fixed peak. Over time, noticing these changes reminds you that the intensity is not permanent.

This method is not common sense because many of us assume that once a bad memory appears, we're stuck with a certain level of discomfort. Tracking the emotional shifts can reveal that intense feelings often come down in a matter of minutes, especially if you engage coping actions. It teaches you that you have influence over the emotional wave, which lowers the sense of helplessness tied to the memory.

Specific "Memory Soothing" Exercises

1. **Controlled Visualization**: Sit in a quiet space, close your eyes, and bring up the regretful memory intentionally. Then, imagine an older or wiser version of yourself stepping into the scene and giving you calm advice. This might feel strange at first, but it can transform the memory from a static replay of pain into a scene that includes compassion or guidance. Over repeated sessions, this controlled visualization can reduce the emotional sting.
2. **Sensory Details**: Some memories are overwhelming because they involve strong sensory details—like the smell of the room, the tone of someone's voice, or the feeling of cold air. If you can recall these details in a safe setting, you start to separate them from the intense regret. You might say to yourself, "Yes, I remember the smell of the coffee and the color of the chairs, but these are just details. They don't control me." This separation can weaken the bond between regret and sensory triggers.
3. **Music or Sound Cues**: Choose a calming piece of music or a sound pattern (like waves or gentle rain) that you associate with relaxation. Play it softly when the memory starts to become too strong. By pairing a stressful recall with a soothing sound, you help the brain link that memory with a calmer state over time. This approach draws from classical conditioning principles, but it's not commonly applied to regret memories in everyday practice.

The Role of Self-Compassion

Even though we avoid certain words by instruction, it is still necessary to address the concept of being kinder to oneself. Overwhelming memories can persist because we refuse to forgive ourselves or allow even a bit of understanding. We replay the event with harsh criticism, insisting, "I should've known better" or "I was so stupid." This repeated punishment keeps the memory active and painful.

To counter this, try a specific mental reminder each time you feel that internal harshness. For example, say to yourself: "I did what I could with the knowledge I had then." This phrase helps you see the context of your old decision, acknowledging that you didn't have the foresight you possess now. Such gentle statements are not about forgetting the mistake; they're about avoiding endless self-lashing that inflames the memory.

Using Physical Objects as Memory Buffers

In some cases, it helps to have a physical object on hand that serves as a "buffer" or a transitional aid when an overwhelming memory strikes. For instance, you could keep a small stress ball or smooth stone in your pocket. When the memory arises, hold or squeeze the object and channel your tension into it for a moment. This might look like a minor trick, but it can produce a small interruption in the emotional feedback loop.

Over time, you can condition yourself so that whenever the memory pops up, your first reaction is to grab the object and perform a short calming exercise. This method is not common sense because people usually think about mental solutions only. By adding a physical anchor, you involve more of your sensory experience, which can effectively reduce the intensity of regretful memories.

When Professional Help Is Needed

Sometimes, regretful memories can merge with deeper emotional wounds, creating a situation where self-help strategies are not enough. If you find that flashbacks are severely affecting your daily life or you suspect symptoms of post-traumatic stress, it may be wise to consult a mental health professional. Techniques like certain forms of therapy, guided exercises, or structured counseling can help process these memories in a safer setting.

It's important to note that seeking help is not an admission of weakness. Rather, it's a step toward resolving a problem that might be too big to handle alone. Professionals have tools to address intense memory-based distress, including methods that help you reframe or desensitize triggers. While you can do plenty on your own, specialized support can accelerate the healing process.

Reclaiming Agency Over Memories

One hidden effect of overwhelming memories is the feeling of losing control. It's common to feel as though the memory runs your mind, rather than the other way around. Regaining a sense of agency involves reminding yourself that you have choices in how you respond when a memory arises. While you can't fully stop memories from surfacing, you can guide what happens next.

For example, you could decide: "If I sense that memory coming, I'll use a breathing exercise right away and then write down one thing I've learned since that event." By planning your response, you change the memory from a sign of doom to a signal for self-help actions. This shift might seem small, but it can build a new mental link: regretful recollections become cues to do something helpful, not just cues for despair.

Avoiding New Regrets Over the Same Memory

Ironically, it's possible to create fresh regrets out of old ones. For example, you might avoid an important meeting because it reminds you of a past failure, leading to new missed opportunities that you later regret. The best way to avoid layering new regrets on top of old ones is to stay aware of how you're responding to triggers. If you notice you're about to skip a crucial event out of fear of re-living a bad memory, pause and consider a small step forward instead.

Adopting a mindset of "controlled confrontation" can help. That is, you don't force yourself into an extreme situation, but you don't hide either. You choose manageable actions that move you a bit closer to facing the memory. This balanced approach prevents a pattern where avoiding regret leads to bigger regrets in the future.

Turning Overwhelming Memories into a Source of Insight

While regretful memories cause pain, they can also reveal details about what you value and how you can adjust your life. If a specific memory keeps haunting you, ask: "What does this memory say about what matters to me?" Perhaps it reminds you of a time you neglected an important relationship, indicating that connections with others are deeply meaningful to you. Or maybe it highlights a moment when you ignored your intuition, showing you the importance of trusting your instincts.

By extracting these lessons, you shift from viewing the memory as mere punishment to seeing it as a guide for better decision-making. This approach can eventually reduce the memory's sting. Each time it appears, you might say, "Yes, that memory is painful, but it also points me to what is important now." Over many repetitions, this reframing can significantly soften regret.

Practical Tips for Daily Use

- **Set Time Boundaries**: Give yourself a limited window each day (like 10 minutes) to consciously think about your regretful memory. Outside of that timeframe, when the memory tries to intrude, gently remind yourself that you have designated a later slot to address it. This can keep the memory from ambushing you at random moments.
- **Breathing Drills**: Practice simple breathing techniques, such as inhaling for four counts, holding for one count, and exhaling for four counts. This calms the stress response tied to sudden memories.
- **Mindful Distraction**: If a memory appears while you're doing something important, briefly switch to a neutral task like tidying a nearby area or counting backward from 50. This interruption can prevent the memory from fully taking over.
- **Sharing Selectively**: Sometimes speaking about an overwhelming memory can help, but be careful with whom and how often you share. Constant retelling can deepen the negative imprint, especially if the listener responds with shock or judgment. A balanced approach is to share with a trusted friend or counselor who can respond thoughtfully.
- **Sensory Kits**: Create a small kit (in a bag or box) with items that help distract or soothe you when a memory hits: a pleasant-scented lotion, a short note of reassurance, a calming photo, or a puzzle book. Having this kit on hand gives you a ready-made set of tools.

Conclusion of Chapter 5

Overwhelming memories tied to regret are not just random flashes of the past. They are shaped by how our minds store emotional events, how we respond to triggers, and the stories we keep telling ourselves. By learning methods like mental reframing, body-based calming, and structured exposure, we can lessen the intensity of these memories without erasing the lessons they hold. The point is not to erase the past, but to ensure that it does not overshadow the present.

CHAPTER 6: REDUCING SELF-BLAME AND ANGER

Self-blame and anger often come as a pair when regret is involved. We might blame ourselves for making a certain mistake and feel anger toward our own actions or toward others who played a role. In some cases, the anger is directed both inward and outward, creating a cycle of frustration, resentment, and deeper regret. This chapter explores ways to recognize self-blame and anger, understand their roots, and use effective strategies to break free from their grip.

Distinguishing Accountability from Self-Blame

One reason self-blame becomes toxic is that it can get confused with taking responsibility. Admitting a mistake is part of maturing. However, taking that awareness too far can lead to self-blame. Self-blame adds elements of personal attacks: "I am worthless," "I always fail," or "I don't deserve another chance." This is not the same as saying, "I made a mistake" or "I can do better next time." The key difference is that self-blame targets your character and identity rather than your actions.

An unusual method to prevent sliding from responsibility into self-blame is to create two columns on paper: "Facts about what happened" versus "Self-criticisms or assumptions." For example, the fact might be, "I missed an important deadline." The self-blame assumption might be, "I am lazy and can never get things right." By separating the data from the emotional statements, you gain clarity. You see that missing a deadline is a factual event, but calling yourself lazy is an assumption that might not be correct. This practice helps you stay in the realm of accountability without descending into personal attacks.

Sources of Anger in Regret

Anger can spring from several places when regret is present:

1. **Anger at Oneself**: You might feel that you let yourself down. This anger can turn into a form of self-punishment, where you think you deserve bad outcomes for your mistake.
2. **Anger at Others**: Maybe someone else influenced your decision or withheld information, leaving you in a regretful situation. You may blame them for steering you wrong or for not giving you the support you needed.

3. **Anger at Circumstances**: Sometimes regret focuses on luck or external events. You might feel bitter that certain opportunities didn't appear or that fate seemed to work against you.

Anger is a potent emotion. It can energize some people to correct their course, but it also can blind them to solutions. When anger lasts, it becomes a barrier to moving on. It is important to notice which type of anger is at play so you can address it in a targeted way.

The Perfectionism–Anger Connection

Many people who regret a past error also hold themselves to a perfectionist standard. When they fail to meet that standard, they become angry for not living up to it. This can be anger mixed with shame. The person feels, "I'm supposed to be perfect, but I messed up." Over time, this anger can bubble into resentment toward other people who appear to meet their expectations or avoid such mistakes.

An uncommon tactic to reduce this perfection-related anger is to set "imperfection goals." For instance, in a minor task such as cooking or exercising, allow yourself a level of performance that is "good enough" rather than flawless. As you practice this in controlled areas of life, you become more tolerant of less-than-perfect results. This tolerance then spreads to bigger situations, lowering the anger that arises when you look back on your own mistakes.

Signs That Self-Blame and Anger Are Linked

Sometimes people don't realize that their anger is actually rooted in self-blame. They may act irritable toward family or coworkers, thinking these individuals are the cause. However, deep down, they're upset at themselves for something they did or didn't do. Recognizing this link can prevent unfair arguments and conflicts.

One sign that your anger might be tied to self-blame is if your frustration flares up when people mention your regret or a topic close to it. Another sign is if you notice a harsh internal voice each time you feel angry, saying something like, "If only you weren't so incompetent, you wouldn't be so mad now." These indicators point to the fact that the anger originates in your own self-directed criticism, rather than an external trigger.

Strategies to Lessen Self-Blame

1. **Reframe Mistakes as Data**: View your regrettable action not as proof of a personal flaw but as a piece of information about what works and what doesn't. For example, if you regret a failed business venture, treat it as data about which strategies were ineffective. Turning mistakes into neutral data can block the emotional spiral of self-blame.
2. **Practice Balanced Self-Talk**: Each time you catch yourself saying something harsh like, "I messed up again," add a balanced statement: "But I learned a valuable lesson." This small adjustment in language can make a large difference over time. It signals your brain that there is more to the story than total failure.
3. **Unpack Childhood Influences**: Self-blame might be a learned habit from early life if you were raised in an environment where mistakes were judged harshly. Reflecting on these roots can help you see that your current self-blame pattern was shaped by past experiences. Recognizing this influence can free you to break the cycle and adopt healthier responses.

Strategies to Tame Anger

1. **Anger Logs**: Keep a simple log where you note when you felt angry, what sparked it, and how you responded. Over time, you might see patterns—such as anger appearing whenever you feel powerless or reminded of your past. Identifying these patterns helps you preempt anger by modifying either the situation or your reaction before the emotion becomes overwhelming.
2. **Physical De-escalation**: Anger can be fueled by physical tension. Actions like squeezing a stress ball, doing quick aerobic movements, or stepping outside for fresh air can help release the tightness in your body. This release often cools the emotional side as well.
3. **Channel Anger Productively**: Sometimes anger is a sign that something needs to change. Instead of turning it into self-blame or attacks on others, focus on a constructive outlet. Perhaps you use that energy to plan a better strategy at work or to address a neglected problem in your personal life. By directing the anger at a solvable issue, you reduce the chance that it will run wild.

Forgiving Yourself Without Dodging Responsibility

Self-forgiveness is often misunderstood. It doesn't mean ignoring or excusing a harmful act. Rather, it means you no longer carry the weight of self-hatred. You recognize what happened, accept the reality of it, and decide to stop punishing yourself mentally. This step is crucial in reducing both self-blame and the anger that can result from regret.

One method is to write yourself a short letter of pardon. In this letter, outline what you regret and why it happened, but also express understanding for the version of you that made the mistake. End with a commitment to act differently in the future. Some find this exercise emotional, but it can be liberating. It's not a magic fix, but it signals to your mind that you are ready to release endless self-blame.

Addressing Anger Toward Others

At times, regret leads us to blame others for their role in our choices. While it might be correct that someone's actions contributed to your situation, holding on to anger can harm you more than them. The question is: how can you acknowledge their part without letting bitterness poison your own life?

- **Clarify Their Level of Responsibility**: Separate your choices from those of the other person. If they misled you or withheld key facts, they deserve a portion of the responsibility. But if you also decided to ignore warning signs or fail to do research, that part is on you. Clarifying who did what can prevent a distorted view where you place 100% blame on someone else.
- **Set Boundaries**: If someone keeps reminding you of your regret or tries to prolong your shame, consider limiting contact or setting clear lines about what you will discuss. This boundary can protect your emotional health and give you space to heal.
- **Consider Constructive Dialogue**: If the relationship matters to you and a direct conversation is possible, calmly express how their actions contributed to your regret and how you felt. This should be done without accusations if possible. Expressing your hurt can be a step toward resolving some of the anger you feel, though it may not always lead to a perfect resolution.Shifting from Anger to Problem-Solving

Lingering anger drains energy you could use to correct or improve your life. A practical way to redirect anger is by focusing on the question, "What can I fix or change now?" This might involve repairing a relationship, revisiting an abandoned project, or seeking new training to correct a past skill gap. By transforming anger into problem-solving steps, you keep it from consuming you.

An uncommon tool here is to compile a "regret fix-it list." In one column, write each regret you feel angry about. In a second column, list possible actions—even small ones—that could reduce the damage or help you move forward. For example, if you regret losing contact with a friend, a fix-it step might be to send a note apologizing for your absence. Shifting your mind from pure anger to actionable tasks often brings a sense of relief and momentum.

Understanding "Anger Debt"

Like financial debt, anger can accumulate over time if you do not address it. Each regretful event adds another layer of unresolved emotion, creating an "anger debt." This can explode if triggered by a small incident, leading to an overreaction that confuses everyone around you. Identifying anger debt requires looking back at multiple regrets to see if they share a common thread—such as feeling unheard, unvalued, or powerless.

Once you see the pattern, you can begin to "pay down" this anger debt by dealing with each piece. That may involve self-forgiveness, apologizing, clarifying misunderstandings, or seeking professional help if needed. The aim is to prevent the burden from piling up further, so you don't keep reacting with disproportionate fury in unrelated situations.

Handling Guilt vs. Shame

Self-blame can include guilt ("I feel bad about what I did") and shame ("I feel bad about who I am"). Anger often spikes when shame is involved, because shame attacks your core identity. Recognizing this difference can help you address the right problem. Guilt can be relieved by making amends or changing your actions, while shame needs a deeper change in how you see yourself.

A method for handling shame is to list positive traits you still have. For instance, you might write, "I made a mistake, but I'm still caring, loyal, and creative." This helps you separate the wrongdoing from your entire being. When you see that you possess good qualities, your shame-based anger may soften, because you start to challenge the assumption that you are wholly flawed.

Dealing with Prolonged Grudges

If you hold a grudge against someone you blame for your regret, that grudge can slowly turn inward, fueling self-blame as well. You might resent them for years, only to realize that your own anger has kept you stuck. To move past a grudge, try thinking about what letting go of the grudge would give you, such as peace of mind, more mental energy, or a chance for new relationships.

A technique that is not widely known in daily practice is to write a "no-send letter" to the person you blame. In it, express your anger, frustration, and sadness—everything you feel. Then decide if you want to discard it or keep it as a private record of your feelings. The act of writing can lessen the mental load of the grudge. It allows you to articulate your grievances without creating fresh conflicts.

The Impact of Self-Blame and Anger on Decision-Making

Excessive self-blame can freeze decision-making. You may worry that any new choice will lead to more regret, so you avoid making any choice. Likewise, anger can push you to make rash decisions, like quitting a job or cutting off relationships. By noticing how these emotions shape your actions, you can spot harmful patterns earlier.

One idea is to apply a "cool-off test" before taking major steps. For instance, if you feel like writing a scathing email or drastically changing your plans, wait 24 hours. Use that time to ask: "Am I deciding from a place of calm thinking, or from a place of self-blame or anger?" If it's the latter, apply some of the techniques above (journaling, breathing exercises, seeking advice) to regain balance.

Apologizing to Yourself

We often hear about apologizing to others, but rarely about apologizing to ourselves. If you realize you have been too harsh on yourself, it might help to speak an internal apology: "I'm sorry for the constant blaming. I'm sorry for not showing kindness to myself." This act can sound odd, but it is a step toward repairing the internal damage caused by self-blame and anger.

After this internal apology, you can pledge to treat yourself better going forward—just as you would promise a friend. This shift helps break the cycle of self-directed negativity, making space for a healthier self-relationship.

Seeking Outside Perspective

If you are lost in self-blame or anger, a trusted outside perspective can be invaluable. This might be a close friend, a therapist, a coach, or a support group. Sharing your thoughts with someone who is not caught up in your regret can bring fresh insights. Sometimes, they will spot positive things in your story that you've missed because you're stuck in negative emotions.

However, be mindful about whom you choose. Some friends may share your anger too strongly or might criticize you more. Aim for someone who can listen with empathy but also offer honest feedback. The goal is not to have your anger or blame validated indefinitely, but to find a balanced view that supports growth and healing.

Building Habits That Counter Self-Blame and Anger

1. **Daily Affirmations**: Simple phrases like "I am allowed to learn from mistakes," "I can grow beyond this," or "My past does not lock my future" can gradually reprogram negative internal scripts. Repetition is key here, even if it feels silly at first.
2. **Scheduled Reflection Time**: Instead of letting blame and anger pop up all day, contain them by scheduling a short reflection period. During that time, write or think about what's bothering you. Afterward, consciously shift focus to more constructive tasks. This practice trains you to manage emotional waves rather than be controlled by them.
3. **Lifestyle Check**: Sometimes, self-blame and anger are amplified by a stressful lifestyle. Chronic lack of sleep, poor diet, or minimal exercise can heighten negative emotions. Improving these areas can indirectly reduce the intensity of regret-related feelings.

Long-Term Outlook

Reducing self-blame and anger is not a quick fix. It involves spotting patterns, adjusting thinking styles, and often revisiting old wounds in a more productive way. Each small step—such as pausing before lashing out, separating facts from assumptions, or channeling anger into a problem-solving plan—chips away at the emotional wall.

As you continue to apply these strategies, you may notice that regretful memories become less charged. The shame or fury that once sprang up so easily might begin to fade. You may still feel pangs of regret occasionally, but they won't have the same power to ignite self-blame or anger. This progress can free you to make decisions more calmly and to see yourself in a gentler light.

Conclusion of Chapter 6

Self-blame and anger are strong reactions that often accompany regret. They can trap you in a cycle of harsh judgment and resentment, prolonging the pain of past mistakes. But by learning to recognize how self-blame differs from healthy accountability, identifying the various sources of anger, and applying targeted strategies to deal with both, you can ease these burdens. Whether through reframing mistakes, practicing balanced self-talk, journaling your frustrations, or seeking outside perspective, there are concrete steps to move toward a state where regret does not control your emotions.

These techniques prepare you for the upcoming chapters, where we will continue exploring different angles of regret. The next sections will expand on understanding what we cannot change, shifting perspective, and shaping future plans that lower the risk of regret. By reducing self-blame and anger now, you create a stronger foundation for the positive actions and mindset shifts that follow.

CHAPTER 7: RECOGNIZING WHAT YOU CANNOT CHANGE

Regret often grows larger when we direct our thoughts and energy toward events or conditions that are beyond our power to alter. Sometimes, people feel trapped, struggling to modify elements of the past that simply cannot be undone. This fixation can fuel frustration and sadness, making it harder to focus on future goals. Learning to recognize what you cannot change is a critical step in easing regret, because it frees you from an unwinnable fight. This chapter explores how to identify unchangeable facts, how to accept them mentally, and how to move forward in a more realistic, healthier way.

Understanding the Limits of Control

Many of us like to think we have complete command over our results in life. While self-determination is important, it is also true that outside forces affect our paths. Economic conditions, family background, health challenges, and social expectations are examples of factors that can shape our choices or opportunities. Recognizing that these external elements exist does not mean becoming passive; it means letting go of the illusion that everything is fully under our authority. This is not a call for inaction, but for clarity about where your influence truly lies.

A practical exercise is to map your regrets, splitting them into two categories: events or choices you had direct authority over, and those significantly affected by forces beyond your reach. For example, let's say you regret failing to land a certain job. If the company shut down due to a sudden economic downturn, your control was less than you realized. That does not mean you had zero influence—you could have tried alternative opportunities—but it highlights that not every outcome was within your command. Seeing these forces at play can reduce undeserved guilt that builds regret.

Why We Resist the Concept of "Unchangeable"

Many people find it hard to accept something as unchangeable. Part of this stems from motivational messages in society that urge us to "never give up" or "keep striving." While determination is commendable in many scenarios, it can mislead us if applied to events that are truly beyond our reach—like something that happened a decade ago or a permanent health condition. Refusing to label anything as "unchangeable" can result in an endless cycle of trying to fix the unfixable, leading to emotional burnout.

Another factor is our own regret-driven thinking. When we focus on what went wrong, we sometimes imagine a perfect scenario in which we fix everything. This can become an emotional loop, as we repeatedly replay the past, believing that if we think harder or "do more," we can alter it somehow. This is a mental trap because the past is not open to correction. Over time, this refusal to accept the unchangeable morphs into deep frustration and blocks constructive steps that could improve our lives now.

Indicators That Something Is Unchangeable

1. **Irreversible Timeframe**: If a regret centers on a period in your life that is far behind you—childhood, teenage years, or a finished school program—then that specific point in time is, by definition, unchangeable. You can still learn lessons from it, but you cannot go back and pick different choices.
2. **Permanent Loss**: If the regret involves someone who passed away or a place that no longer exists, you cannot recreate the exact circumstances. You might honor their memory or find ways to honor what was lost, but you cannot restore the exact situation.
3. **Physical Limits or Nature**: Certain physical facts cannot be undone. For instance, if you regret not being taller or regret an injury that changed your body in a lasting way, you might adapt or look for treatments, but you cannot turn back the clock to a completely different body structure.
4. **Legal or Official Constraints**: Sometimes regrets involve official matters—like missing a legal deadline, losing a license, or passing a strict cut-off date for an application. Once the official rules finalize the outcome, you cannot reverse it.

Recognizing these markers can help you avoid wasting effort trying to adjust unchangeable facts. Instead, you can dedicate your energy to what remains within your influence.

The Emotional Weight of Trying to Change the Unchangeable

People often spend large amounts of emotional energy wrestling with regrets tied to impossible changes. For instance, a person might regret not telling a deceased parent how much they cared, replaying that scene in their mind, wishing for one more conversation. That regret can evolve into deep sorrow because there is no future interaction possible with that parent. While the regret and sorrow are understandable, the ongoing attempt to mentally "fix" it is futile.

Over time, this stress can lead to mental fatigue and physical problems, such as disturbed sleep or ongoing anxiety. The constant mental loop steals attention from daily life, hurting relationships with people who are still here and with new opportunities. Identifying that certain regrets fall into the "unchangeable" category can reduce this burden by allowing a different response—one that respects the reality of the situation.

Shifting from Unchangeable to Meaningful Acceptance

Acceptance does not mean you like or endorse what happened; it means you acknowledge the finality of certain events. This shift frees mental space. Instead of demanding change from the unchangeable, you can explore how to carry the lessons forward. For instance, if you regret not apologizing to someone who has passed away, you might direct your remorse into becoming more thoughtful about how you handle current relationships. The regret becomes a signal for how you want to behave going forward.

One helpful technique is to write a "final statement" regarding the unchangeable event. In it, describe the regret clearly, note why it cannot be altered, and state what you plan to do about it mentally. For example: "I regret missing the chance to say goodbye to my friend before she moved away forever. I cannot rewrite that event because she has already settled in a new country and we lost touch. From now on, I will stay aware of important farewells and be proactive about communicating my feelings." This written statement can serve as a reference point when your mind drifts back to trying to reverse the past.

Dealing with Residual Longing

Even after acknowledging what is unchangeable, you may still feel longing. This is normal because it reflects the part of you that wishes things had gone differently. Instead of denying or burying this emotion, you can transform it into a mindful reflection. For example, you might allow yourself five minutes a day to feel that sadness about the missed chance. But when those five minutes end, you shift focus to a constructive task. This approach honors your emotional truth while preventing it from dominating your entire day.

Another method is to create a symbolic act of closure. If you regret not pursuing a musical talent in your youth, you might set up a small ceremony where you write down that regret and place it in a box. Then you store the box or discard the note as a gesture of moving on. This act does not magically remove all sadness, but it signals to your mind that you have recognized the regret's unchangeable nature and are choosing to stop wrestling with it.

External Pressures to Change the Unchangeable

Sometimes, friends, family, or even popular culture may unintentionally encourage you to fix something that cannot be fixed. They might say, "It's never too late," or "You can always do something about it." While these statements often come from a place of kindness, they can compound your internal conflict if the regret truly falls outside your control. It's important to respond gently, letting them know that you have identified the boundaries of the situation.

For instance, if you regret not having a different educational background and someone insists you can just go back to college, maybe your personal circumstances (age, health, financial constraints) make that impossible. Standing firm in your recognition of reality can keep you from chasing illusions and can help you look for realistic solutions. That might mean finding online courses that provide some of the knowledge you wanted, or focusing on a related skill that is still feasible.

How Accepting the Unchangeable Affects Relationships

When you stop pouring energy into changing the unchangeable, you often become more present for loved ones. You are less distracted by internal battles and more able to connect with others. Furthermore, people around you sense when you have gained peace about past regrets. It can reduce tension in the household if you used to be moody or withdrawn because of an unresolvable regret.

In addition, this acceptance can improve your ability to empathize with others who also feel stuck. You might share what you learned about letting go of impossible tasks and focusing on feasible goals. While everyone's regrets are unique, seeing another person find calm in the face of unchangeable events can be inspiring and can open conversations about healthy coping strategies.

Rethinking "Impossible" Situations

Sometimes, a regret might seem unchangeable at first glance, but on closer inspection, partial remedies may exist. For example, you might regret failing an exam that prevented you from entering a certain job field. You cannot go back in time to change that result, but you might research alternate paths or certifications in a related field. This does not negate the regret that you did not enter that original field, but it opens a door to a different solution. Recognizing the difference between true unchangeability and partial alternative routes can shape a more balanced view.

Still, it is vital to stay honest about which parts are fixed and which parts allow flexibility. If you hold to the hope of changing a factor that is firmly in the past, you might delay trying new directions. For example, you may cling to the idea that the exam board will retroactively adjust your score, which is extremely unlikely. Recognizing the firm boundary between reality and wishful thinking stops you from wasting time, energy, and emotional bandwidth on an unrealistic outcome.

Handling Regrets Tied to Relationships

One of the hardest forms of regret involves relationships—especially those that ended badly or ended because of factors like distance or death. You might think, "If only I had tried harder," or "If only I had been more understanding." When such a relationship is gone for good, you cannot recreate or repair it in the same way. This truth may be painful, but seeing it as final can help you focus on preserving or improving the relationships you do have.

It can also lead you to acknowledge changes you can make in your behavior, so you do not repeat the same mistakes. For instance, if you regret never reconciling with a parent who passed away, you might apply that lesson by staying closer to siblings or checking in more often with older relatives. You learn to avoid that same regret in another form. This approach does not erase the original regret, but it can reduce its sting by translating it into meaningful actions now.

When Regret Involves Health or Physical Changes

Sometimes regrets revolve around not taking care of health or not preventing an injury. If the condition is irreversible, you might grieve the loss of certain abilities or the ease you once had. Yet continuing to blame yourself for a permanent situation does not restore your health. Instead, it can block you from finding adaptive ways to manage your condition or from finding new possibilities in your life.

An approach is to focus on what you can do with your body as it is now. For example, a person who regrets damaging a knee might discover different forms of exercise that do not strain that joint. Or someone who regrets not eating well for years might still create better habits to slow further damage. By balancing what cannot be changed (past neglect) with what can (current and future choices), you build a practical path forward.

The Risk of Overgeneralizing "Unchangeable"

There is a potential pitfall in accepting the unchangeable: you might start labeling everything as unchangeable, including events or habits that you do have the power to affect. This happens if you swing too far in the other direction. It's crucial to differentiate between events that are truly locked in the past and ones that still have a margin of possibility. For instance, if you regret how you handled your finances last year, that time period is gone, but your financial habits now can be adjusted.

To avoid overgeneralizing, review each regret individually. Ask, "Is there any realistic step I can take to shift the outcome in the present or future?" If yes, then it's not fully unchangeable. You can focus on those actions. If no, then it belongs in the category of acceptance. By doing this careful check, you keep from giving up on areas where progress is still possible.

Strategies to Anchor Yourself in the Present

Once you identify the parts of your regret that are unchangeable, you can support your mental health by grounding yourself in what is happening now. Some helpful ideas include:

- **Sensory Focus**: Periodically stop what you are doing and notice the sights, sounds, and smells around you. This shifts your mind from the past to the present physical environment.
- **Daily Goals**: Start each day with one or two realistic objectives. This practice keeps you anchored in actions that you can take now, reminding you that the present is where change can occur.
- **Scheduled Reflection**: Give yourself a specific time each week to reflect on past regrets, but limit it. Outside that time, if your mind drifts back, remind yourself that you have a planned slot for such thoughts.
- **Skill Building**: Focus on learning or improving a skill that is relevant to your life today, whether it's professional or personal. This growth-oriented activity shifts mental energy away from impossible changes and toward achievable goals.

Personal Identity and the Unchangeable Past

Many regrets revolve around who we used to be—our younger selves, who might have been less aware, more impulsive, or less considerate. While we cannot erase that version of ourselves, we can recognize that personal identity is not fixed in time. We continue to evolve, and our old mistakes do not have to define us forever. A practical exercise is to write a letter to your past self, acknowledging mistakes but also noting how you have grown since then. This can reinforce the idea that you are allowed to move beyond old errors.

Finding New Meaning in the Shadow of Regret

Even an unchangeable regret can hold seeds of meaning if you examine it from a different angle. For instance, perhaps the regret led you to be more compassionate toward others who faced similar issues. Or it inspired you to support a cause related to your past mistake, helping others avoid a similar outcome. By investing energy in these positive directions, you reshape the role that the regret plays in your life. It's no longer just a source of pain; it becomes part of a broader context that leads to constructive actions.

Breaking the Cycle of Obsession

For some individuals, regrets about the unchangeable become an obsession. They constantly replay scenarios, trying to figure out if there was a tiny missed option. The mind loops through "what if" questions, refusing to accept the finality of what happened. Recognizing this loop is the first step to breaking it. Techniques like thought-stopping or mild aversion therapy (such as lightly snapping a rubber band on your wrist each time you notice the loop) can help you interrupt these patterns. The goal is not to punish yourself but to create a signal that halts the negative cycle before it spirals too far.

Seeking Support When Acceptance Is Difficult

Some regrets are tied to deep wounds—like abuse, betrayal, or significant loss. Acceptance can be overwhelming, and you might need outside help from a counselor, support group, or mental health professional. These sources provide guidance for unpacking trauma or intense sorrow that might accompany your regret. They can offer tools to process those emotions safely, which can eventually lead to a form of acceptance that does not feel like giving up but rather setting yourself free from an unresolvable past.

Conclusion of Chapter 7

Recognizing what you cannot change is a pivotal step in handling regret. Although it may sound straightforward—after all, the past is the past—many people become stuck trying to rewrite events that are permanently set. Understanding the boundaries of your control and clearly labeling which regrets fall outside those boundaries can ease mental strain and open space for healthier growth. By accepting the finality of certain events, you grant yourself permission to focus on the present and future. This shift allows regret to serve as a source of wisdom rather than an endless cycle of frustration.

CHAPTER 8: METHODS TO SHIFT YOUR PERSPECTIVE

Perspective shapes how we see the world and interpret our experiences. When regret takes hold, our viewpoint can become narrow or negative. We might see ourselves as failures, or believe life has treated us unfairly. Shifting perspective is a powerful way to reduce regret's hold. This chapter presents detailed methods to encourage healthier thinking, drawing on uncommon techniques, mental exercises, and daily practices that counteract the distorted outlook regret often creates.

Why Perspective Matters in Regret

Perspective is more than just attitude. It's the mental framework we use to process events, define our role in them, and anticipate future outcomes. When we stay locked in a regretful viewpoint, we often emphasize personal shortcomings or missed chances. This can lead to a distorted sense of identity, overshadowing the strengths and successes we do have. In shifting our viewpoint, we can see a more balanced picture, which helps us recognize positive opportunities and accept mistakes without letting them dominate.

Challenging Automatic Beliefs

Many regrets come with automatic beliefs, such as "I'm unworthy" or "I'm always behind everyone else." These ingrained statements can trigger strong emotions and direct us toward self-defeating patterns. To shift perspective, it's key to question these beliefs:

1. **Spot the Source**: Track when a negative thought arises. Maybe it appears after you see someone else's success or recall a past failure. Identifying the trigger helps you realize this belief is not an absolute truth but a habit linked to certain circumstances.
2. **Test the Evidence**: Ask yourself, "Is there real proof that I'm always behind?" Often, you'll find exceptions. Maybe you achieved something significant recently, or you excel in another area. Finding these contradictions weakens the hold of the negative belief.
3. **Replace or Reframe**: After identifying a false assumption, craft a more balanced statement. For example, "I have made mistakes, but I've also

grown in ways that matter." This new statement reorients your viewpoint from total negativity toward a realistic middle ground.

The Technique of Mental Distance

Sometimes regret is deeply personal, making it hard to see the situation objectively. An uncommon technique is to practice mental distance. Pretend you are an observer or a friend giving advice. Instead of saying, "I messed up," you might phrase it as, "Person A encountered a setback in a project." Although it feels strange, this shift from first-person to third-person language creates a small gap, reducing the intensity of self-criticism. It can help you see the situation with greater clarity, as though you are advising someone else.

You can also try visualizing your regret on a small screen in your mind, as if you were watching a short scene rather than reliving it from the inside. This mental trick can reduce emotional intensity. Over time, practicing mental distance can help you respond to regret with more calmness and a wider perspective.

Expanding Your Timeline

Regret often narrows our sense of time, trapping us in the moment of the mistake or missed chance. To break this pattern, consider an expanded timeline:

- **Past-Present-Future Reflection**: Write a brief outline of your life up to now, focusing not only on what you regret but also on moments of achievement or happiness. Then, imagine and outline some potential future milestones. Visualizing your life story this way can lessen the weight of a single regret. It reminds you there is more to your existence than that one event.
- **Long-Term Forecast**: Ask, "Will I still feel this regret five or ten years from now?" Often, the answer might be, "It will fade," especially if you take steps now to grow and adapt. Projecting forward in this way can reduce the urgency and heaviness of your current regret, helping you see it as one part of a bigger picture.

Gaining Perspective from Multiple Angles

We tend to view our regrets from a single angle—our own. Shifting perspective can mean seeking alternative angles to see the same event. For example:

1. **Others' Input**: Ask a trusted friend or family member how they see your regretful situation. They might point out overlooked factors or strengths you showed. Their external viewpoint can balance your harsh self-judgment.
2. **Opposite Scenario**: Imagine the reverse situation. If your regret is not speaking up, picture a scenario where you did speak up but it led to a negative outcome. This thought experiment can highlight the idea that any decision could result in multiple possible regrets. Realizing this can reduce the sense of a perfect "lost" scenario.
3. **Different Cultural Lens**: Sometimes, reading about how people in other cultures handle similar setbacks can shift your perspective. For instance, some cultures see mistakes as normal steps on the path of growth, rather than personal failures. Learning about these differences broadens your mental framework.

Finding Humor as a Perspective Tool

Humor may seem out of place when discussing regret, but it can be a strong way to shift perspective. This does not mean mocking yourself or ignoring the seriousness of a mistake. Instead, it involves spotting life's absurdities and allowing a little bit of lightness. For example, if you regret a time you embarrassed yourself in public, think about how humorous that situation might be from a comedic angle. Laughter or mild amusement can ease tension, helping you see that even embarrassing events can become small anecdotes in the grand scheme of life.

One technique is to think, "How would a comedy movie portray this regretful moment?" This approach can lessen the emotional charge. Once the emotions cool, you can analyze the event more sensibly. Though not common in serious self-help instructions, humor is a valid coping tool for perspective shifting.

Adopting a Growth Mindset

A growth mindset treats mistakes and failures as material for learning. Instead of labeling yourself as incompetent, you view errors as hints on how to improve. Shifting to this mindset can dramatically reduce regret's weight. For instance, if you regret a failed relationship, a growth mindset reframes it as a chance to discover which communication styles or boundaries did not work. This is not naive positivity; it is a systematic way to see data in your experiences.

To apply this:

- **List What You Learned**: For each regretful event, jot down at least two or three lessons, no matter how small. Make them concrete, like "I learned that I need clear communication early on in a partnership."
- **Plan Future Actions**: Decide how you will use these lessons. For example, "Next time I enter a relationship, I will discuss core values in the early stages." This plan transforms regret into a teacher for your next steps.

Perspective-Shifting Through Service

Another less common method for gaining perspective is through acts of service or volunteering. When we are stuck in regret, we often focus primarily on our own distress. Shifting your attention toward helping others—like reading to elderly people, cleaning a local park, or mentoring youth—can provide a new viewpoint. You see that life is bigger than your single regret, and you might gain a sense of purpose that softens self-focused sorrow.

Regular service also introduces you to individuals from different walks of life, broadening your appreciation for varied experiences and challenges. It can foster gratitude for what you do have. This shift does not trivialize your regret, but it places it within a wider human context, often reducing the feeling of isolation or hopelessness.

Physical Movement and Perspective

It might not be obvious, but physical movement can aid in shifting perspective. Activities like hiking or taking a brisk walk can clear mental fog, spark new thoughts, and break stagnant thought cycles. Even simple stretching routines or short exercise breaks during the workday can lift your mood. A slight mood boost might be enough to help you see your regret differently.

If you're open to a more structured approach, try "mindful walking." While walking slowly, notice each footstep, the feel of the ground, and the tension in your legs. This focus on the present can quiet the noise of regret in your head. With that quietness, fresh insights may emerge.

Imagining the Best-Case Scenario

Sometimes, regret focuses on the worst-case "what if." You might think, "If I had made this move, my life would be perfect now." But is that necessarily true? It can help to imagine the best possible scenario if you had chosen differently, then brainstorm realistic downsides it might have involved. For example, maybe you regret turning down a job offer that sounded glamorous. Envision the bright side: a higher salary, an exciting new city. Then also consider the challenges you might have faced: high living costs, a competitive environment, or less free time.

By balancing the potential positives with possible negatives, you gain a more even view. This process helps you realize that every path has trade-offs, reducing the fantasy that a single different choice would have solved all problems. It widens your perspective to see that your actual life path may include benefits you overlooked while dwelling on regret.

The Power of Questions

Shifting perspective can be aided by asking unusual questions about your regret:

- **"What hidden advantage might I have gained from that regretful event?"**
  Maybe you built resilience, empathy, or even practical know-how.
- **"Who might I help because I went through that experience?"**
  Sometimes, your past mistakes can guide you in mentoring others in similar situations.
- **"What about my present life would not exist if I had chosen differently?"**
  You might have never met a specific friend or developed a certain skill.

These questions break the mental rut of focusing solely on the negative side of regret. They challenge you to look for unexpected positive angles.

Reframing Words and Language

Our word choices reflect and shape our perspective. Terms like "failure," "disaster," or "ruined everything" can fix our mindset on negativity. Switching to more neutral or constructive language helps you see events in a broader light. For example, instead of "I failed completely," you might say, "Things did not go as

I hoped." This smaller shift in phrasing can ease the emotional blow and help you view your regret as a setback rather than an irreversible catastrophe.

Using Art and Creative Outlets

Artistic expression—like painting, writing fiction, or playing a musical instrument—can facilitate perspective changes. When you create something, you're blending feelings, imagination, and problem-solving. You might discover you can express aspects of your regret in ways that bring new insight. For instance, writing a short story where a character faces a similar regret can help you see your situation from another angle. This creative distance can reveal solutions or acceptance that were not apparent before.

Rotating Priorities

Sometimes, regret stems from the feeling that we poured energy into the wrong priority. By rotating your current priorities, you can shake up your perspective. For example, if you regret not taking time to travel (while avoiding the forbidden word), you could assign a higher priority to small weekend trips or new local experiences now. Or if you regret missing out on a particular hobby, dedicate a few hours a week to exploring it. When you shift your present priorities, you demonstrate to yourself that you are not stuck forever in the same pattern. This can reduce the feeling that regret has permanently dictated your path.

Perspective in the Face of External Opinions

Others' opinions can shape our viewpoint, sometimes fueling regret if they suggest we made a terrible choice. While it's wise to consider feedback, it's also important to establish your own perspective. If you find yourself constantly bending under someone else's negative commentary, step back and ask: "Does this person truly understand my whole situation? Are they qualified to judge my choices?" You might realize they are speaking from limited information or their own biases. This realization can allow you to adopt your perspective more confidently, limiting regret fueled by external viewpoints.

Avoiding the "Reverse Halo" Effect

The "halo effect" is a known bias where one positive trait or success outshines everything else, leading us to judge someone or something too favorably. A "reverse halo" can also occur, where one negative event or trait overshadows all positive aspects. Regret can cause this effect in our self-evaluation: one regretful act becomes the lens through which we see our entire identity. Recognizing this helps you see that you are more than your regret. Perhaps you have strengths, accomplishments, and relationships that do not connect with this single event. Breaking the "reverse halo" fosters a broader, kinder self-view.

Step-by-Step Perspective Shift Plan

1. **Identify the Core Regret**: State it plainly, such as, "I regret not pursuing that business idea."
2. **Name the Automatic Thought**: Observe what you usually tell yourself, like, "I'm a failure because I missed a big chance."
3. **Question the Thought**: Ask, "Is that always true? What are some things I have done well?"
4. **Find a New Narrative**: Write a short paragraph that offers a balanced view: "I missed one chance, but I have succeeded in other ways. I can still explore different business ideas or learn from that missed opportunity."
5. **Visualize a Wider Lens**: Picture your life story over several decades, placing this regret in a larger timeline to see it as one event among many.
6. **Revisit Periodically**: Each week, read your new narrative and compare it to your old perspective. Notice if you feel less weighed down by regret over time.

When Perspective Shifts Don't Stick

Sometimes, despite these methods, the negative perspective bounces back. This can be due to deeper emotional wounds, or habits built up over years. In such cases, professional guidance may help. Therapy or counseling can provide structured exercises, accountability, and emotional support. It's not failure to seek help; it's a sign of commitment to real growth.

Additionally, remember that perspective shifting is not a one-time action. It's an ongoing practice. You may need to repeat certain steps or mix several techniques until a shifted viewpoint becomes your default. Even then, some regrets might pop up at stressful times, so it's wise to keep these methods in your mental toolkit.

Conclusion of Chapter 8

Shifting perspective is a powerful approach to easing the weight of regret. By questioning entrenched beliefs, practicing mental distance, expanding your sense of time, and exploring different angles—through creativity, humor, service, or seeking outside viewpoints—you can reshape how you interpret your past. This does not erase regret, but it changes its place in your overall life story. Instead of seeing a regret as a defining failure, you begin to view it as one part of a broader narrative that includes learning, success, and ongoing growth.

With the methods in this chapter, you are better prepared to loosen the grip regret can have on your self-image and daily thoughts. As you move to the next chapters, you will find more tools for using regret as a catalyst for wise future decisions and for learning how to find effective ways to plan ahead. By coupling acceptance of unchangeable events (from the previous chapter) with a flexible, open perspective, you create a stable foundation for lasting progress.

CHAPTER 9: PLANNING FOR FUTURE DECISIONS

Regret often comes from decisions we look back on with sadness or disappointment. By preparing for new decisions more carefully, we can lower the chance of making choices that cause lasting remorse. This chapter will explain how thoughtful planning, self-awareness, and practical tools can help you make decisions with fewer regrets. It draws on techniques from psychology, risk assessment, time management, and everyday observations to shape a wiser decision-making process.

Why Future Planning Matters

When we do not plan well, we often act on impulse or rely on emotional reactions that may be strong at the moment. Then, once the situation changes, we might regret those quick moves. Good planning does not remove all risk, but it helps us foresee possible problems and weigh our options with greater balance. It also gives us room to rethink or adjust decisions if we see warning signs.

A well-designed planning approach helps break patterns of regret. If your past regrets involved financial missteps, then studying better budgeting methods or consulting experts before making big purchases could be part of your planning. If you previously regretted not exploring career options, building a habit of information-gathering and networking can shift how you approach choices.

Facing the Difference Between Impulse and Clear Thought

We all have impulses—instant desires to do something that feels satisfying right now. While there is nothing wrong with spontaneity in harmless contexts, impulse can lead to regret when it shapes life-changing decisions. For instance, rushing to quit a job after a bad day might feel liberating at the moment, but it can spark serious regret if you do not have an alternative lined up.

A practical tool to separate impulse from reason is the "24-hour rule." If you feel strongly about a decision that can wait, pause for a full day. Return to it after that pause and see if you still feel the same way. This practice can prevent regrets fueled by short-lived emotions like anger, infatuation, or panic.

Setting a Clear Purpose for Each Decision

Some decisions have many layers—financial, emotional, social. Often, regret arises when we act without clarifying the main purpose behind a choice. For example, if you are deciding whether to move to a new city, ask yourself what the top reason is: career growth, better quality of life, or family obligations. Once you define the purpose, you can assess your options more effectively.

A helpful exercise is to draft a small "purpose statement" for big decisions. Write down: "The main goal of this decision is…" and fill in the blank. Keep it clear and specific. This statement becomes a reference point. If an option does not support that main goal, it may not be the best path. This clarity often prevents regrets tied to getting sidetracked by minor temptations or outside pressure.

Analyzing Risks and Potential Payoffs

When planning for decisions, many people overlook the systematic assessment of risks versus payoffs. They might focus on short-term gains or only fear the worst outcome. Balanced decision-making means considering both the potential upsides and the realistic downsides:

1. **List Possible Outcomes**: Imagine a few likely results if you proceed with a certain choice. For example, if you plan to invest money in a new business idea, list out best-case, moderate-case, and worst-case scenarios.
2. **Assess the Probability**: For each outcome, give a rough estimate of how likely it is to happen. Even if it is just a guess, this process forces you to think about the odds. Maybe the best-case scenario is less likely than you hoped, or the worst-case scenario is not as probable as your fear suggests.
3. **Weigh Emotional Costs**: Regret is not only about losing money or time. It also can result from emotional tolls. If a decision might strain important relationships or require you to compromise strongly held values, that risk is significant. Factoring in emotional costs can prevent regrets later.

Using a structured risk-payoff approach can slow impulsive decisions and help you see the broader picture. You are less likely to end up saying, "I never thought about the potential downsides," which is a common root of deep regret.

Research and Gathering Information

Knowledge is power when it comes to avoiding regret. A lack of information often leads us to make guesses that backfire. If you regret past choices made hastily or with incomplete facts, building a solid research habit can be a game-changer.

- **Broad Reading and Learning**: If you are about to switch careers, read articles, books, and case studies on that field. Talk to people already doing the job. If you are considering a major purchase, compare prices, read reviews, and check user experiences. The more you know, the less chance you have of being blindsided by unforeseen details.
- **Talking to Experts**: Sometimes a short chat with a specialist can save you from massive regrets. This can be a financial advisor, a legal consultant, a mental health expert, or even someone with years of practical experience in a certain area. Many people skip professional input to avoid costs or because they feel rushed. However, a mistake from poor research can be far more expensive or painful.
- **Crowdsourcing Cautiously**: Online forums, social media groups, or acquaintances can offer varied perspectives. But remember that not all advice is good advice. Some opinions may be based on limited knowledge. Use crowd input as a starting point but verify important facts through reliable sources.

Time Management in Decision-Making

We often regret choices we made under time pressure. When the clock is ticking, we might select an option just to move on, only to realize later we did not think it through. While not every decision can wait, it is wise to allow yourself enough time for bigger ones. Arrange your schedule so that major decisions do not coincide with major life changes or deadlines. If you must decide quickly, try to still follow a condensed version of the steps in this chapter—looking at goals, potential outcomes, and verifying critical facts.

Decision Diaries and Patterns

A "decision diary" is a log where you record the reasoning behind big decisions before you finalize them. You note your expectations, your main reasons, and any concerns you have. Later, you can check this log to see how accurate your predictions were. Over time, this reveals patterns about how you decide. Maybe you notice that you often rush if you are stressed. Or you might see that certain advice sources consistently give poor guidance.

Maintaining a decision diary requires discipline, but it can be extremely helpful. Not only does the act of writing slow you down to think more carefully, but reading it later can teach you how to improve. This reduces regret because you learn from each decision, even if the outcome was imperfect.

Consulting Trusted People (But Staying True to Yourself)

Family, friends, or mentors can provide new angles on a decision. However, you remain the person who has to live with the choice. If their advice feels off for your personal situation, it is okay to go a different direction. Sometimes people wind up with regrets because they followed advice that clashed with their gut sense of what was right. Balancing outside advice with your own judgment can protect you from regrets caused by living someone else's plan.

A strong approach is to gather outside opinions after you have done your own research and reflection. Then compare their suggestions to your personal priorities. If they align, great. If not, see if they raise points you missed. If you still disagree, trust your own process. This approach helps you avoid regrets caused by blindly following others or ignoring valuable feedback.

Small Trials Before Big Moves

If possible, test out a decision on a smaller scale before fully committing. For example, if you think you want to change careers from teaching to programming, try taking a short coding course or working on a small project first. This mini-test can reveal whether you truly like the work, saving you from quitting your teaching job prematurely and facing regret if the new path does not fit.

Such small trials give you real-world information. Theory is one thing, but actual experience can reveal details that were not clear before. By gathering evidence through experiments or trial phases, you lower the risk of regret because you have "previewed" the decision before locking it in.

Knowing Your Values

Regret often involves a conflict between our actions and our core values. When we do something that violates an important personal principle—maybe honesty, compassion, or loyalty—it can lead to deep regret. Clarifying your values before making choices is a way to ensure alignment. You can ask, "Does this decision match what I stand for?"

One practical method is listing your top three to five values. Then, for each major decision, check if the choice helps or hinders those values. If you see a big mismatch, that is a red flag. Acting against your own values can generate powerful regret later, even if the decision seems profitable or convenient in the short term.

Watching Out for "Sunken Cost" Thinking

The "sunken cost fallacy" is when you stick with a bad decision just because you have already invested time, money, or effort. You might say, "I've already spent a year on this project, so I can't quit now." Yet, continuing might lead to bigger losses. People often regret not cutting their losses sooner. Good planning means looking at a decision based on current facts, not past investments. Ask yourself, "If I were not already involved, would I still choose to do this?"

Recognizing the sunken cost fallacy can save you from regrets linked to doubling down on a poor path. Instead, you can redirect energy to a more promising direction. While letting go can be difficult, it is sometimes the wisest action if you see that a certain plan is no longer viable.

Practical Tools for Structured Decisions

1. **Pros-and-Cons List**: This is classic, but it can still be useful. The key is to be thorough, including intangible factors like emotional well-being.
2. **Scoring System**: Assign a numerical value (like 1 to 5) for important criteria: potential financial gain, alignment with values, stress impact, etc. Sum the scores to see which choice ranks higher. This method can remove some emotional bias.
3. **Worst-Case Scenario Planning**: List what would happen if everything went wrong. How would you cope? Could you recover? Sometimes seeing that you can handle the worst helps you move forward without regret.

Other times, you realize the worst is far worse than you are prepared to deal with.
4. **Time-Chunk Tests**: If uncertain about a decision, set a limited period to try it. For example, "I will try living in the new city for three months," or "I will test this marketing method for four weeks." Evaluate after that period, adjusting as needed.

Emotions vs. Logic

Logic and emotion are not enemies. Both have a role in decisions. Pure logic might ignore passions that make life meaningful, while pure emotion can ignore real-life constraints. Balancing them helps reduce regrets. If you notice that your emotions are too intense—maybe you're extremely excited or extremely upset—take a step back. Wait for emotional equilibrium, then review the facts. Conversely, if you're only looking at spreadsheets and ignoring how you feel, that could also cause regret if the choice goes against your deeper nature. Finding balance allows you to honor both factual analysis and genuine desire.

Building a Supportive Environment

Your environment can shape how you plan decisions. If you surround yourself with people who encourage impulsive actions or unrealistic thinking, regret might follow. Seek out relationships and settings that support wise decision-making. This might mean joining a professional group focused on your area of interest or staying close to friends who foster rational debate. Over time, this supportive environment can become a safety net, catching you when you might otherwise rush into a regrettable choice.

Learning from Past Decision Patterns

Most of us have repeating patterns. Some people realize they regret decisions made under peer pressure. Others see they regret decisions made in anger. By pinpointing these triggers, we can address them before the next choice. If peer pressure is a problem, you might plan to talk with a neutral friend or mentor first. If anger is an issue, adopt a cooling-down routine or a no-decision policy while in a rage. This self-awareness, combined with action steps, is how we grow beyond old habits and avoid repeating regrets.

Accountability and Reflection

If you are serious about preventing regret, put an accountability system in place. This can be a friend or a partner who checks in with you about major decisions. Tell them your plan and ask them to question your motives or assumptions. Having someone you trust reflect your thoughts back to you can reveal blind spots. You might also schedule a monthly reflection session for yourself to review ongoing decisions, see if you are drifting off course, and make corrections early.

Timing and Seasonality

Some decisions are influenced by seasonal trends or specific times of the year. For example, certain industries have hiring surges at specific months, or real estate markets shift with the seasons. Planning decisions around these patterns can give you better choices and reduce regrets. If you push a choice at a bad time (like buying property during an inflated market), you risk regret once conditions change. A bit of research on seasonal or cyclical factors can help you find the right moment.

Handling Decision Fatigue

Decision fatigue occurs when we have to make too many choices in a short span. The mental energy required to process each decision builds up, resulting in poorer judgments later. This can lead to regret, as we might snap at the final decision of the day without proper review. To manage this, group routine decisions or simplify choices where possible. For example, decide on a weekly meal plan in advance rather than facing daily meal decisions. Reserve your mental energy for significant decisions. This helps prevent regrets caused by a tired mind making hasty calls.

Building Confidence in Your Planning

Confidence in decision-making does not mean overconfidence. It means you trust that you have done your homework, thought through your values, and prepared for possible outcomes. This calm confidence reduces regret because you know you made the best decision you could with the available information. Even if the outcome is not perfect, you can adapt without feeling that you blindly leaped. This sense of trust in your process is reassuring when facing the unknown.

Long-Term Vision and Flexibility

While planning aims to reduce regret, life is unpredictable. Even the most well-researched decision can lead somewhere unexpected. Maintaining a flexible mindset allows you to adjust without harsh self-criticism. If you realize partway that a decision is not going as planned, the willingness to pivot can save you from bigger regrets. This does not mean giving up at the first sign of difficulty—it means staying open to new data and responding accordingly.

Your long-term vision acts like a compass. Even if a few decisions are off course, you can still move closer to the bigger goals. By clarifying what you hope your life to look like in five or ten years, you maintain direction. Each decision becomes a step that either aligns with that direction or signals the need to reconsider. When you look back, you will more likely see a chain of thoughtful actions that reflect genuine effort to avoid needless regret.

Conclusion of Chapter 9

Planning for future decisions is a key element of regret prevention. By balancing emotional and rational thinking, setting clear goals, consulting trustworthy sources, and experimenting with smaller steps first, you reduce the chance of being caught off guard. Creating habits like a decision diary, a consistent research process, and a mindful review of values ensures that your choices reflect who you are and where you want to go. While no method can guarantee a perfect outcome every time, this structured planning lowers the probability of regret. It gives you a grounded confidence that you have done your due diligence, allowing you to meet the future with greater calm and fewer "if only" moments.

CHAPTER 10: UNCOVERING PRACTICAL WAYS TO LEARN FROM REGRET

Regret can be paralyzing if we let it control our thoughts without learning anything from it. However, regret also holds valuable lessons for those willing to face it more directly. In this chapter, we will examine how to extract real insights from regret rather than letting it remain a source of constant pain. We will look at concrete exercises, reflective techniques, and a few unexpected strategies that transform regret into a teacher, helping you make better choices and grow in self-awareness.

Why It Is Crucial to Learn from Regret

Learning from regret ensures that your past mistakes or missed opportunities are not wasted. Instead of simply wishing things were different, you gather meaningful clues about how to approach life going forward. For instance, if you regret a business endeavor that collapsed, taking the time to understand the missteps can help you launch a stronger venture later. Ignoring regret or hiding from it is a missed chance to refine your judgment and adapt your behavior.

Moreover, learning from regret can reduce its emotional weight. When you see that regret led you to take positive steps, you become less likely to view it as a pointless burden. It shifts the narrative from "I messed up badly" to "I learned something significant, and I am changing my path." This viewpoint promotes long-term resilience and self-confidence.

Reflecting on Mistakes in a Structured Way

One reason regret lingers is that we only reflect on it in a shallow or repetitive manner, often with harsh self-criticism. Instead, use a structured approach:

1. **Write a Summary**: Begin by describing the regretted event in plain language. Include what happened, who was involved, and any relevant context.
2. **List Contributing Factors**: Ask yourself, "What factors led to this outcome?" These might be internal (like impatience, fear, or poor communication) or external (like an economic slump, a conflict in scheduling, or bad timing).

3. **Pinpoint the Key Errors**: Focus on what you could have influenced. Maybe you did not gather enough information, or you acted purely out of emotion. Identifying these key errors is more constructive than lumping everything under "I failed."
4. **Extract the Lessons**: For each key error, articulate a takeaway. For instance, "I should have tested the business model with a pilot program before spending large sums." Keep these lessons concise and actionable.
5. **Plan a Do-Over**: If you were to face a similar situation again, what steps would you change based on your new insights? Write a short plan that corrects the old mistakes.

This structured reflection interrupts the loop of self-blame. It gives your mind specific tasks—figuring out what went wrong, why, and how you can do better next time. That is how regret transitions from a nagging thought into a source of growth.

Spotting Hidden Patterns

Sometimes, regretful events share a common thread. A person might regret several different relationships but notice later that all of them ended for similar reasons—maybe lack of honest communication or jumping into commitments without enough thought. By comparing multiple regrets side by side, you can spot patterns that might remain invisible if you consider each regret alone.

Create a chart of your top three or four regrets. List the circumstances, your behaviors, and the outcomes. Look for repeated red flags: "Rushed decisions," "Fear of rejection," "Impulse spending," etc. Once you notice a pattern, you can target that behavior in your future approach to decisions. Patterns often indicate a default habit—maybe you avoid confrontation or you follow the crowd. Recognizing and addressing these habits is a direct way to reduce repeated regrets.

Turning Regret into a Tool for Empathy

One less obvious benefit of regret is that it can sharpen your empathy for others. When you suffer regret, you understand how painful it is to feel you missed a vital chance or harmed someone. This awareness can help you connect with people facing similar remorse. You might offer a listening ear or share what you learned, creating bonds that help both you and them feel less alone.

In professional settings, empathy drawn from regret can make you a more effective leader or team member. If you regret past mistakes in managing employees, you can empathize when a coworker struggles. Instead of judging them harshly, you might recall how you felt in a similar situation, guiding you to give supportive feedback or second chances. This shift might not be common sense, but it can elevate the emotional tone of any environment.

Using Regret to Improve Emotional Regulation

Regret often triggers strong emotions such as sadness, guilt, or anger. These feelings, while uncomfortable, can teach emotional regulation skills if you tackle them mindfully. Observe how regret affects your body—does your heart race, do your muscles tighten, do you experience shallow breathing? Recognizing these physical cues is a first step toward calming down before you act on anger or despair.

Learning how to name your emotional states precisely—feeling "tense," "ashamed," "disappointed"—can help you avoid being overwhelmed. This process is sometimes referred to as building "emotional granularity." Once you identify the exact emotion, you can apply specific coping strategies, like slow breathing, muscle relaxation, or a quick walk. Over time, these emotional regulation skills will help you handle regretful thoughts with less drama.

Reconsidering Missed Opportunities

Many regrets involve opportunities not taken—such as not going to a certain school, not learning a skill, or not confessing feelings to someone important. While you cannot recover the exact moment, you can sometimes seek a new but similar opportunity. For instance, if you regret never traveling to a certain region when you were younger, perhaps you can plan a shorter or adjusted trip now. Or if you regret not learning a language, you can start studying it, even if you're older.

Taking action to address a missed opportunity in a new form not only lessens regret but also introduces fresh possibilities. It is a reminder that life is often more flexible than we assume. While it is not the same as turning back time, it can still lead to partial satisfaction and open doors. In some cases, the alternative you explore might turn out to be just as meaningful as the original plan would have been.

The Role of Self-Compassion

Self-compassion means treating yourself with the same kindness you would offer a friend who feels regret. People who lack self-compassion tend to bury regret in self-criticism and shame, which blocks learning. When you approach your mistakes with empathy toward yourself, you calm the defensive part of your mind that wants to deny or run from regret. This state allows you to look at facts more objectively and see a path for growth.

Practical steps for building self-compassion around regret include:

- **Gentle Self-Talk**: When regret surfaces, speak inwardly as a kind mentor. "Yes, it's painful that I made that choice, but I can learn and do better."
- **Recalling Past Improvements**: Remind yourself of other times you stumbled but then adapted. This helps you remember that errors are not permanent dead ends.
- **Balance**: Acknowledge that mistakes are a normal part of being human. You are not uniquely flawed for having regrets; you are part of a shared human experience.

Creating a Regret "Laboratory"

Imagine having a personal laboratory where you examine regret without the emotional baggage. You take a memory of a regretted event and break it down like a researcher. Ask:

1. **Hypothesis**: "If I had done X differently, would the outcome have changed?"
2. **Variables**: List the factors that were at play: time, place, people's actions, your mood, financial constraints, etc.
3. **Test**: Think about alternative actions you could have taken. Would they have realistically been possible or beneficial?
4. **Conclusion**: Summarize what you discovered about how much control you had and what was truly out of your hands.

This method helps you refine your sense of control and see regret as data for your "research" on yourself. Over time, your "laboratory reports" can build a clearer picture of how you operate under stress or in uncertain conditions. Rather than letting regret fuel negative self-images, you collect insights that guide future improvements.

Documenting Lessons in a Personal Handbook

After analyzing regrets, it's useful to record your lessons somewhere you can review them quickly—like a "personal handbook." Each time you learn something from a regret, write a short paragraph. For example, "Lesson from regret about not speaking up in meetings: People might actually appreciate hearing my views. Next time, I will raise my hand early." Organize these by theme (communication, finances, relationships, health). When facing a fresh decision, skim through the relevant section of your handbook to recall what your past self discovered. This structured approach prevents you from forgetting insights or repeating the same regrets due to forgetfulness.

Balancing Realism and Optimism

Learning from regret requires a balance of realism and optimism. You must be realistic about what went wrong and how you contributed. Pretending you had no part in the outcome blocks learning. At the same time, you need optimism that you can apply those lessons. If you sink into fatalistic thinking—believing you're doomed to repeat mistakes—nothing changes. Realism ensures honest analysis; optimism fuels the willingness to implement improvements.

A good exercise is to write two lists after exploring a regret. One list, "Realistic Challenges," details the hurdles that might appear if you try a new approach next time. The second list, "Reasons for Hope," highlights resources, personal strengths, or supportive people that can help you succeed. By keeping both lists in front of you, you remain grounded yet motivated.

Rewriting the Internal Narrative

Regret can create an internal narrative that might say, "I'm the person who ruined that big chance" or "I'm always behind because of that one slip-up." If left unchallenged, this story can shape your identity in a negative way. Rewriting the narrative is a deliberate act. Instead of "the person who ruined the chance," you could say, "the person who made a tough mistake but gained valuable lessons to share with others." While it sounds small, this re-labeling changes your self-perception. You shift from a stuck viewpoint to one that sees value in the experience.

Sharing Lessons with Others

Talking about regret is not always easy, but sharing the lessons you drew from it can be enlightening for both you and the listener. This might happen in informal conversation, group discussions, or even through writing blog posts or articles. By explaining how you turned regret into insight, you clarify those insights further for yourself. Also, hearing outside perspectives can deepen your understanding. Someone might say, "That resonates with my own mistake, but here's an angle you might not have considered." These exchanges can solidify the new lessons, reducing the chance you will repeat the same error.

Adopting a "Learning Challenge" Mindset

A "learning challenge" is when you set a short-term goal to apply a lesson from regret in a real scenario. For example, if you regret never networking enough in past jobs, set a 30-day challenge to attend one professional event or schedule coffee with a new contact each week. Keep track of your experiences. Did you feel awkward? Did you discover something valuable? Document it. By framing it as a challenge, you turn learning from regret into an active pursuit rather than a vague intention. This can accelerate change and reduce future regrets about "never trying."

Learning from Regret in Relationships

Regrets in relationships—like harsh words, betrayals, or neglect—can be some of the hardest to face. The lessons here often revolve around communication, empathy, and boundaries. For instance, if you regret lying to a partner, you might learn the importance of honesty even when it's uncomfortable. If you regret letting someone repeatedly disrespect you, you might learn to set firmer boundaries sooner. Relationship regrets can be especially instructive because they show how our actions (or inactions) impact others.

A specific tip is to practice role-play scenarios with a trusted friend or counselor. If you regret a past argument with a family member, play out how you might handle a similar conflict differently. This helps you embed the lesson in a more vivid way, preparing you for real situations. It can be awkward at first, but the hands-on practice makes it more likely you will recall and use the lesson when tensions rise again.

Handling Regret That Cannot Be Fixed

Certain regrets are tied to irreversible outcomes. Even so, you can learn from these experiences in ways that might guide your behavior in future settings. If you regret never saying goodbye to a deceased loved one, you can still practice being more present for the people in your life now. If you regret a permanent health setback caused by negligence, you can still adopt healthier habits going forward and possibly educate others about prevention. While the specific event cannot be fixed, the lesson remains valuable, and it can prevent further pain for yourself or those around you.

Checking for Overcorrection

Sometimes, in trying to avoid repeating a regret, people swing too far the other way. If you once regretted trusting someone who deceived you, you might become overly suspicious of everyone. If you once regretted missing out on an opportunity, you might chase every new possibility until you burn out. Overcorrection can create a fresh set of regrets. Stay balanced by monitoring whether your new behavior is making your life better or if it's pushing you into another extreme. This awareness prevents you from replacing one regret with a different one.

Ongoing Self-Audit

Learning from regret is not a one-time event. Consider an ongoing self-audit schedule. Every month or quarter, review new regrets or old ones that are still relevant. Ask if you are applying the lessons you identified. It is common to slip back into old habits after the initial motivation wears off. Regular check-ins ensure you stay aligned with your growth plan and keep refining how you handle similar decisions.

Conclusion of Chapter 10

Regret can serve as an extraordinary teacher if we treat it as raw material for learning rather than a permanent emotional burden. By reflecting on mistakes in a structured way, spotting hidden patterns, showing self-compassion, and proactively seeking ways to rewrite our internal stories, we can turn regret into a catalyst for wiser action. Each lesson gleaned reduces the chance of repeating the same misstep and strengthens our overall life strategy.

Though it takes effort to face regrets honestly, doing so frees us from being stuck in a painful loop. By designing practical methods—like a personal handbook, a regret "laboratory," or targeted learning challenges—we give ourselves a roadmap for continuous growth. This approach respects both the reality of our past errors and our ability to move beyond them. In the chapters ahead, we will build on this foundation, exploring how to strengthen mental habits, handle outside pressures, and reshape regret into something constructive for the future.

CHAPTER 11: BUILDING STRONGER MENTAL HABITS

Regret often intensifies when our daily mental habits are unsteady or overly negative. We may recognize regret in specific situations, but sometimes the deeper issue is how we think and respond every day. When a person establishes healthy mental routines, they become better able to handle regretful thoughts before those thoughts grow out of control. This chapter shows how to develop more balanced thinking patterns, regulate your mood, and stop small concerns from turning into big regrets. By focusing on small, repeatable practices, you can build a mental framework that supports resilience and self-trust.

Why Mental Habits Matter for Regret Management

Mental habits are like daily routines in our minds: how we talk to ourselves, respond to stress, handle criticism, or approach challenges. If these routines are harmful—like automatically blaming yourself, worrying about everything, or assuming the worst—the effect on regret can be huge. Each time you make a minor mistake, a harmful habit might amplify it into a major source of sadness.

On the other hand, strong mental habits can buffer you from regret. Instead of ruminating on a small error, you might quickly identify the lesson and move on. Instead of harshly judging yourself, you might frame the mistake with measured thinking. Over time, this difference in daily approach reduces regret's power.

Habit Loop Basics

Research on habit formation often highlights a loop: **cue → routine → reward**. While this framework is typically used for physical habits, it applies to mental ones as well:

- **Cue**: A certain trigger prompts a thought process. For instance, spotting a social media post about someone's success might become a cue for self-comparison.
- **Routine**: You engage in a learned response, such as negative self-talk or envy.

- **Reward**: There is a short-term effect—maybe feeling self-pity or anger that feels somewhat familiar. This "reward" might not be healthy, but it reinforces the habit.

To break a negative mental routine, you can replace it with a more constructive response. For instance, if the cue is "seeing someone's success," the new routine might be "focus on your own progress," and the reward becomes "feeling motivated instead of regretful." Identifying cues is crucial because it allows you to intervene before negative thoughts spiral.

Mindful Transitions Between Tasks

A practical way to build better mental habits is to pay attention to transitions throughout the day. We often carry emotional baggage from one activity to the next. For example, if you had a tense meeting at work, you might still be upset when you sit down to answer emails, leading to hasty replies that cause regret. By pausing for 30 seconds between tasks—closing your eyes, taking a slow breath, and mentally releasing the previous event—you reset your mood. This quick "reset" habit prevents small stresses from piling up, lowering the chance of regretful actions spurred by lingering frustration.

Positive and Negative Thought Balancing

Some people think they must be perpetually positive, but that can lead to ignoring genuine issues. Others dwell too much on negativity, seeing only problems. A balanced approach recognizes both. An exercise to achieve this is:

1. **Identify a Current Concern**: Maybe you are worried about a work assignment.
2. **List the Negatives**: Write them down briefly. Example: "I feel unsure about how to approach the project."
3. **List the Positives**: For the same topic, list any opportunities or supportive factors. "I have a supportive teammate, and I have access to training materials."
4. **Summarize the Middle Ground**: Combine both lists into a simple statement: "I'm facing challenges, but I have resources that can help."

This practice trains your mind to avoid extremes. Over time, you form a mental habit of weighing pros and cons rather than falling into regretful thinking patterns.

The Power of Micro-Affirmations

Micro-affirmations are tiny statements you say to yourself to reinforce confidence or calm. Unlike grand affirmations ("I am perfect!"), micro-affirmations are more subtle and realistic. For example: "I am capable of figuring this out," or "I can handle new challenges, step by step." Repeating one or two micro-affirmations when you feel regret creeping in can ground you.

What's not common sense is the importance of matching the affirmation to your real context. If you say something too grand, you might not believe it, causing mental pushback. Micro-affirmations that match actual facts—like your previous successes or your ability to learn—have a stronger impact on your daily mindset.

Small Daily Challenges

It is helpful to set a small mental challenge each day. This might be resisting the urge to self-blame, noticing three things that went well, or calmly talking through an issue instead of ignoring it. These small challenges build discipline in your thought processes. Similar to how you might train a muscle by doing daily exercises, you reinforce mental strength by meeting small challenges. Over time, these regular efforts add up to a robust habit system.

Handling Unexpected Triggers

We cannot always predict what the day will throw at us—traffic jams, rude comments, sudden disappointments. These unexpected triggers can quickly set off negative patterns if we are not ready. One approach is to have a mental "emergency plan." If you feel your stress or regret response rising, take a moment to do a brief grounding practice:

- **Name the Trigger**: Silently say, "I am upset because this person cut me off in traffic."
- **Label the Feeling**: Note your emotion: "Frustration rising, feeling of unfairness."
- **Engage a Calming Action**: A few slow breaths or a quick mental shift to a calm image.

This sequence can be practiced mentally so it becomes a habit. By repeating it during small triggers, you get better at handling larger ones, which in turn prevents regretful outbursts or decisions driven by anger.

Constructive Self-Talk Scripts

Crafting "scripts" for common scenarios is another hidden gem for building strong mental habits. Suppose you often regret how you respond to criticism. You could create a simple script: "When someone criticizes me, I will pause, thank them for the input, and say I want to think about it before responding." Rehearse this script mentally. Then, when criticism happens, your brain has a prepared path: pause, thank, reflect, respond. This approach shields you from impulsive words or defensive reactions that lead to regret.

Scripts can be adjusted for different areas: conflict resolution, dealing with mistakes, turning down requests. They act as mental shortcuts, helping you stay composed and consistent under pressure.

The Impact of Media Consumption on Mental Habits

We often forget that what we watch or read shapes our mental routines. Constant exposure to negative news or social media feeds can increase worry, envy, or regret. One lesser-known practice is to set clear limits on how and when you consume media. For instance, some people choose to read news only once a day at a set time, or they avoid scrolling social media right before bed. This simple boundary can make a big difference. By controlling the flow of external stress, you keep mental space clear for healthier habits.

Building a Resilience "Playlist"

Music, podcasts, or uplifting audio clips can be woven into your day to support stronger habits. Some people create a short playlist of calm or inspiring content to play during transitions—such as driving home from work—to shift out of a stress mindset. Hearing certain words, stories, or even soothing music regularly can become a mental cue that says, "Now I shift into a calmer, more balanced state." Though not everyone uses this tool, it can be a powerful method to stabilize emotions and counter regretful thinking.

Daily Wins Journal

A daily wins journal is a small notebook or digital file where you write down small victories each day. These wins do not have to be dramatic—they can be as simple as "Completed my to-do list" or "Reached out to a friend who needed help." The act of recording small successes shifts your focus from regrets or failures to progress. Over time, you train your mind to notice positive moments instead of fixating on negative ones. This does not ignore real problems; rather, it balances them with achievements you might otherwise overlook.

Using "If-Then" Planning

"If-then" statements allow you to plan how you will react in certain conditions, which strengthens mental habits. For example, "If I start feeling guilty about the past, then I will quickly do a breathing exercise and recall one lesson I learned from that event." This clear cause-and-effect approach helps you jump into constructive action instead of brooding. By forming multiple if-then statements for different regret triggers—financial worries, relationship stress, performance anxiety—you create a roadmap that your mind can follow without overthinking.

Accountability Buddy System

Sometimes, working on mental habits alone feels isolating. An accountability buddy can help. This person could be a friend, coworker, or someone from an online group. You share your goals for mental habit change—like reducing negative self-talk or practicing calm responses—and agree to check in regularly. The buddy might ask how many times you used a calming technique that week or if you recorded any wins in your journal. Knowing someone will ask can motivate you to stay consistent. It also offers a chance to acknowledge small improvements together, reinforcing the new habit loop. Stepping Away from Perfectionism

Perfectionism can trigger regret because the minute something falls short, we dwell on what could have been. A useful habit to counter perfectionism is "deliberate imperfection." For example, if you are writing a short email, allow a tiny, harmless error, like not polishing every sentence to perfection. Observe your discomfort and remind yourself that people rarely notice. This small exercise trains your mind to accept that minor flaws do not necessarily lead to disaster. Over time, this reduces the anxious mental loop that fuels regret over tiny missteps.

Building Emotional Vocabulary

When regrets arise, they often come with strong feelings. Many people only label these feelings as "bad," which is too vague. Expanding your emotional vocabulary helps you identify the exact state: is it "disappointment," "remorse," "sadness," or "confusion?" Each label points to a different strategy. For instance, disappointment might call for adjusting unrealistic expectations, while remorse might lead to making amends if possible. By practicing naming emotions, you sharpen the mental habit of responding more accurately, reducing the spiral of regretful thoughts.

Creating a Personal Reminder Board

Sometimes we forget the mental habits we want to strengthen. A personal reminder board—on a wall, in a small notebook, or even a digital note—can display short messages or keywords: "Pause," "Breathe," "Check facts," "Small wins." Placing this board where you see it daily (like near your desk) keeps these triggers fresh in your mind. Each time you glance at it, you reinforce the new habit pattern. This approach prevents the slip back into old, regret-inducing habits, because you have a constant prompt to recall your new mental routines.

Embracing Adopting Calm in Conflict

Regret often surfaces after heated conflicts where we say things we wish we could take back. Building a habit of calm conflict resolution can break that pattern. You might practice a short method: when a conflict starts, mentally say, "I am open to hearing the other side before reacting." Then, consciously slow your breathing and focus on listening. This small shift from reacting to listening can interrupt the pattern of impulsive remarks. Over time, you create a self-image as someone who handles disputes methodically, reducing the likelihood of regretful outbursts.

Turning Reflection into Routine

Reflection is more than just thinking about your day. You can build it into a scheduled practice. For example, at the end of each week, spend 15 minutes reviewing any regrets, triumphs, or areas of confusion from the past days. Ask yourself: "Did I use my planned mental habits? When did I slip? How can I improve next week?" By turning reflection into a consistent event on your calendar, you ensure gradual progress. Without routine reflection, mental habits fade or become inconsistent, making it easier for regret to return unchecked.

Addressing Self-Doubt Directly

Self-doubt is a silent factor in regret. People who doubt their abilities might fail to take needed risks, leading to regret for missed chances. Or they second-guess every decision, fueling regret soon after making a choice. A helpful habit is daily "skill check." Write one skill you used well that day—did you organize a meeting smoothly, or provide useful feedback to someone? Recognizing your competencies daily quiets self-doubt. This is not arrogant or naive; it is a factual look at what you did competently. Over time, this habit builds confidence, which reduces regrets linked to indecision or excessive fear.

Rotating Mental Exercises

Humans get bored doing the same drill every day. To keep mental habits fresh, rotate them. One week you focus on balanced thinking exercises, the next week on emotional labeling, the following week on micro-affirmations. This rotation keeps your brain interested and engaged. It also broadens your skill set, ensuring you have multiple ways to handle regret triggers. In the long run, a variety of mental tools help you adapt to changing situations without falling into old harmful routines.

Rewards That Reinforce Good Habits

While intangible rewards like better self-esteem are great, you can also set small external rewards to reinforce new mental habits. After a week of consistent practice, treat yourself to something modest—like an hour reading a fun book or a relaxing bath. This is not about overindulgence but about linking a sense of payoff to your discipline. The brain often responds to tangible rewards, even small ones, by strengthening the new habit loop. By systematically rewarding your progress, you encourage yourself to keep going, which lowers the chance of regret creeping back in.

Reviewing Long-Term Impact

Finally, remember that building stronger mental habits is a long-term strategy. The immediate effect might be subtle—maybe you cut down on a small portion of daily self-blame—but over months, this can significantly reduce regret. Each healthy habit you adopt weaves into your broader outlook, making you more stable during setbacks. When you look back a year later, you may see fewer episodes of regret-driven anxiety, because your mind has learned to handle stressors in a balanced way.

Conclusion of Chapter 11

Strengthening mental habits is a foundational step in preventing and managing regret. By paying attention to daily patterns—how you talk to yourself, how you react to triggers, and how you approach challenges—you reduce the chance of letting small mistakes balloon into major regrets. This chapter's strategies, from mindful transitions and micro-affirmations to "if-then" planning and emotional labeling, offer practical ways to reshape your internal processes. Over time, these small changes add up, creating a stable mental framework that handles regretful events more calmly.

A resilient mindset does not come from a single breakthrough. It is the product of repeating healthy thought routines until they feel natural. This gradual shift in your mental landscape can transform the way you handle past regrets and reduce the odds of future ones. As you move forward in this book, keep these habit-building tips in mind, since they connect directly with the next topics: handling outside pressures, managing emotional self-care, and eventually shaping a life less burdened by regret.

CHAPTER 12: STRATEGIES TO HANDLE EXTERNAL PRESSURES

Regret can arise not only from our internal thinking but also from outside influences. Society, workplace demands, family expectations, and peer opinions can all press us into choices we later regret. This chapter focuses on how to recognize and manage external pressures so they do not trap you in decisions or paths that conflict with your values. By learning to spot and deal with social, cultural, and professional constraints, you can reduce regrets caused by trying to fit into someone else's mold.

Understanding Where External Pressures Come From

External pressures often come in subtle forms. It might be a friend's casual remark that pushes you to feel behind in life. Or a workplace policy that forces quick decisions, leaving you with little time to think. At times, family traditions can steer you down a route that does not align with your interests. Recognizing these sources is the first step to avoiding regret. Pay attention to when your stress or hesitation spikes in reaction to someone else's words or an institution's rules.

It is not always about blame. Sometimes, others do not realize how their suggestions or expectations affect you. Employers might believe strict deadlines are necessary for productivity, not sensing how that restricts your process. Family members might offer advice out of genuine concern, without knowing it conflicts with your personal goals. By identifying these dynamics, you can begin to address them in a firm but respectful way.

The Social Comparison Trap

Comparing ourselves to peers, siblings, or social media figures is a powerful form of external pressure. We might regret not having the same achievements or lifestyle. One tactic to limit this pressure is to "audit" your social comparison triggers. For one week, note any moment you feel that surge of envy or inadequacy after seeing someone else's success. Then, reflect on whether that feeling truly aligns with your own values. Ask, "Do I actually want what they have, or am I just responding to the hype?" Often, you will realize the source of pressure is more about social perception than genuine desire.

You can also adjust how you interact with social media. If you follow accounts that consistently make you feel lacking or that push you to unrealistic standards, consider unfollowing or muting them. This is not running away from reality; it is controlling your environment so that outside comparisons do not constantly feed regret. Over time, removing these triggers can help you see your own progress more clearly.

Workplace Pressures and Setting Boundaries

Many regrets arise from workplace decisions—taking on too many tasks, tolerating unfair treatment, or ignoring personal limits. Handling workplace pressure involves setting boundaries. This might mean talking with your manager about realistic workloads or politely declining extra projects if you are already at capacity. Fear of job loss or missing future promotions can push people to accept every demand, but that often leads to burnout and deep regret later.

A hidden strategy is to keep a private "work diary." Write down what tasks you accept, why you accepted them, and how you feel during the process. This log can reveal patterns where you say "yes" out of fear or habit rather than real interest. By seeing these patterns, you can plan a calmer response. For example, you might practice a phrase like, "I'd be glad to help, but let me check my current workload first." This small routine can prevent regrets that come from over-commitment.

Cultural and Family Expectations

In some cultures, certain life paths—like getting married at a young age, entering a family business, or pursuing a specific profession—are strongly promoted. People who follow these paths without questioning them might later regret not exploring their own interests. It is tricky, because family bonds are important. However, living against your true self to please relatives can create long-term sadness.

One approach is open communication: if you feel pressured to follow a path you do not want, speak honestly and politely to your family about why you have different goals. Show that you respect their views but still need to find your own direction. This can lead to conflict, but it is often less painful than silently building resentment that leads to big regrets. In some cases, compromise might be possible—fulfilling certain family roles in a limited way while carving out space for what you truly want.

Peer Influence on Life Choices

Friends and peers can shape our decisions in subtle ways. Maybe they push for expensive outings or certain lifestyle choices. If you join in just to fit in, you may regret the financial strain or the mismatch with your own personality. Checking your motivation is key: "Am I doing this because it aligns with my happiness, or am I afraid of missing out or losing acceptance?" Some fear that disagreeing with the group will cause social isolation. But true friendships often allow for differences.

A practical step is to offer alternatives. If your group always chooses costly nights out, suggest a cheaper activity you genuinely enjoy. Observe the reaction. If they remain open and flexible, you can still spend time together without regret. If they insist on their ways and pressure you, it may be time to expand your social circle. This shift can be uncomfortable, but it reduces regrets tied to living by other people's rules.

When External Advice Conflicts with Your Instinct

People in our lives often give advice—some of it good, some of it ill-suited for us. Deciding which advice to accept requires self-awareness. If you sense a strong inner reluctance about someone's suggestion, pause. Ask yourself whether your reluctance is fear-based or value-based. Fear-based reluctance might deserve a second look (sometimes stepping outside your comfort zone is good). But if your gut feeling says the advice contradicts who you are, ignoring that feeling can lead to regret.

A technique for evaluating advice is to imagine each piece of guidance playing out in your life. Visualize the likely outcome. Notice whether you feel a sense of alignment or a sense of conflict. This quick mental test might sound basic, but it can reveal hidden tensions. After all, your future is shaped by the choices you make today, not by what others think should happen.

Dealing with Criticism and Expectations at Work

External pressure also comes in the form of criticism from bosses or peers. While constructive feedback can help you grow, negative or unfair criticism can steer you toward regretful choices—like giving up too soon or changing your style just to please others. Learn to distinguish between constructive feedback (which points to real, actionable areas of improvement) and destructive feedback (which is vague, personal, or insulting).

If your job demands changes that contradict your values or well-being, it is worth weighing the long-term costs. Some folks remain in toxic work settings out of fear, only to regret the lost years. Others abruptly quit without a backup plan, causing a different regret. A middle path is to assess your resources, update your résumé, network discreetly, and look for better options if needed. Having a plan reduces the regret of a snap decision while keeping you from staying in a harmful environment too long.

Media Sway and Public Opinion

In today's era, public opinion can form quickly online. People fear making mistakes that could bring a wave of criticism on social platforms. This fear can push them to avoid risks, remain silent about important issues, or mold their identities around external acceptance. Over time, living for public approval can cause deep regret if you stifle your real voice or moral stance.

One strategy is to define your own code of conduct. Write down what you believe in and what you are willing to stand for publicly. If the online crowd disagrees, at least you know your position is grounded in conscious thought rather than chasing popularity. This does not mean ignoring all feedback, but it means not shifting your entire identity for the sake of virtual praise. By anchoring your sense of self, you reduce regrets caused by trying to please an unpredictable public.

Constructive Disobedience

Sometimes, the best path is to defy an external pressure that is harmful or unjust. People who blindly follow rules or norms they see as misguided might regret it deeply later. Constructive disobedience means thoughtfully pushing back or seeking alternatives. For example, if a workplace policy leads to unethical outcomes, you might gather like-minded colleagues to propose changes or, in severe cases, blow the whistle. While this is not simple, it can save you from regrets about staying silent. Knowing you acted on principle, even if it brought challenges, often brings more long-term peace than quiet compliance with something you know is wrong.

Identifying Emotional Blackmail

Emotional blackmail is when someone uses your feelings of guilt, fear, or obligation to push you into actions that serve their interests over your own. Examples include a friend who says, "If you were truly loyal, you'd do this for me," or a family member who threatens to cut ties if you do not follow their plans. Recognizing these tactics is important. People under emotional blackmail often make regretful decisions because they act out of fear of losing the relationship.

The best response is setting clear boundaries. Calmly state, "I understand your viewpoint, but I am not comfortable doing that. I still value our relationship and hope we can find a middle ground." Such a statement asserts your stance without cutting people off automatically. If they continue to use threats, you may need to create distance for your own well-being. Though this is painful, it can prevent deeper regrets of living under manipulation.

Building an Internal Compass

An "internal compass" is a set of personal principles that guide choices when external pressures arise. This compass might revolve around honesty, respect, growth, faith, or any other key ideals. When faced with a decision pressed on you by outside forces, you refer back to this compass:

1. **Is it true to my values?**
2. **Does it help me grow or protect my well-being?**
3. **Does it respect others in a healthy way?**

If a demand or suggestion fails these simple tests, it is likely to produce regret later. By practicing this mental check, you filter out external pressures that conflict with your personal code.

The "Pause and Check" Method

Similar to "if-then" planning, "pause and check" is a rapid method to stop yourself from bending to sudden pressures. When someone demands something or tries to influence you quickly, you respond with a neutral statement: "I need a moment (or a day) to think it over." Then you check with yourself or trusted advisors. This small pause can save you from regretful yes-or-no answers made purely under heat or intimidation. Over time, others may learn you are not someone to push around spontaneously.

Guilt Traps and Obligations

Society and culture often build guilt traps—like the idea that you must attend every family event or fulfill every custom. While traditions can be meaningful, not every tradition aligns with every individual's life. Skipping a family gathering might cause short-term tension, but if attending it consistently leaves you drained, you might regret the time lost for your own needs. Weigh the cost of guilt from saying "no" versus the regret of saying "yes" to something that truly goes against your personal well-being. Sometimes, a polite decline is healthier. If you feel compelled to explain, do so honestly but briefly. Over-explaining can fuel arguments or further pressure.

Educating Yourself to Reduce Manipulation

External pressure sometimes takes advantage of your lack of knowledge. Whether in business deals, contracts, or social issues, people may pressure you to sign or agree quickly. The more you educate yourself, the less vulnerable you are. For instance, if you face financial pressure from salespeople, learn basic finance or negotiation tips. If you face social pressure to adopt a certain belief, read diverse viewpoints before committing. Knowledge is a shield against regrets caused by being rushed or misled.

Handling Groupthink

Groupthink occurs when members of a group go along with an idea without critical analysis, often to maintain harmony. If you sense groupthink in your social circle, workplace, or community, you might regret staying silent if the group's choice leads to a bad outcome. One way to counter groupthink is to play the role of the respectful skeptic. Ask pointed but calm questions: "Have we considered other perspectives?" "What data supports this plan?" This not only protects you from regret but can also help the group avoid flawed decisions. If the group resents your questions, that may be a sign you need to reconsider your association with it.

Social Contracts and Fair Exchanges

We live within various social contracts—unspoken agreements about how we should behave, such as neighbors helping neighbors or colleagues covering each other's tasks in emergencies. Recognizing these social contracts is important, but so is ensuring the relationship remains balanced. If you give help constantly and never receive any in return, resentment and regret can grow. Politely requesting fairness in these exchanges is not selfish; it maintains healthy boundaries. This mindset keeps you from feeling trapped in one-sided obligations that later turn into regret.

Emotional Safety in Relationships

External pressures from romantic partners can be intense, especially in relationships where one partner tries to shape the other's choices. Pay attention to red flags like attempts to control your career, friendships, or beliefs. If you yield to these pressures, you could regret losing your identity. Trustworthy relationships allow you to be yourself without constant fear of disapproval. If someone consistently pushes you to be a version of yourself that feels wrong, consider seeking professional counseling or, if needed, ending the relationship. It is better to address this early than to look back with regret on years spent living under someone else's dominance.

Building a Support System

Sometimes, resisting external pressure is easier if you have a supportive community. This can be friends, a professional group, a counselor, or an online community that shares your values or goals. Knowing that others back you up can make it simpler to say "no" to unwanted demands. For instance, if your family pressures you to follow a certain path, having mentors or friends who respect your chosen route can balance that pressure. This support system serves as a reminder you are not alone, preventing regrets like "I gave in because I had no one else to turn to."

Reflecting on Consequences Before Acting

External pressures often rush us into actions without letting us think about outcomes. A quick mental exercise is to project yourself a few months or years ahead. Ask, "If I do what they want, how might I feel later?" or "If I refuse, what might happen?" This forecasting approach provides a clearer picture of potential regrets. Sometimes the long-term regret of complying is greater than the short-term discomfort of refusal. By spending just a few minutes imagining future scenarios, you sharpen your decision-making and can resist pressure in a more reasoned way.

Conclusion of Chapter 12

External pressures come in many shapes, from cultural expectations and workplace demands to peer influences and emotional blackmail. Any of these can lead to regret if you follow them blindly against your values or needs. Recognizing these pressures is the key to handling them in a way that minimizes regret. Tools like boundary-setting, open communication, "pause and check," building knowledge, and connecting with supportive networks help you assert your own path while still maintaining important relationships when possible.

By learning to spot the difference between constructive advice and manipulation, between a healthy challenge and an unreasonable demand, you preserve your sense of self. This sense of self is vital for reducing regrets tied to living someone else's plan. As we move forward, the next chapters will show how to use emotional self-care, turn regret into constructive insights, and manage other challenges so that the regret we do face can be transformed into lasting wisdom rather than ongoing sorrow.

CHAPTER 13: IMPROVING EMOTIONAL SELF-CARE

Emotional self-care is the act of supporting your inner well-being through consistent and purposeful activities. It addresses the feelings and thought patterns that shape your mental state every day. When regret weighs heavily, emotional self-care becomes crucial because it protects you from drowning in negative thoughts. This chapter explores how to form a stable emotional center, maintain calm in the face of stress, and encourage inner stability. By strengthening your emotional self-care routine, you reduce the chance that regret will take over your life.

---

1. Understanding Emotional Self-Care

Emotional self-care means making choices and practices that preserve or increase your mental resilience. It is more than just a way to "cheer up." Rather, it is about noticing your emotional condition, understanding how it affects your life, and consciously meeting those emotional needs. When done well, emotional self-care helps you adapt to challenges and handle regrets without becoming overwhelmed.

For example, if you have a pattern of ignoring sadness, it might transform into deeper frustration. Embracing consistent emotional self-care—such as letting yourself cry once in a while, discussing problems openly, or taking a break when overwhelmed—stops those emotions from turning into toxic stress. Through regular self-care, you become more aware of early warning signs that regret is building up, and you can respond before it grows out of control.

---

2. Balancing Work, Personal Time, and Rest

Many regrets surface when people feel stretched too thin. They might regret not spending enough time with family or regret passing up personal hobbies for work demands. Achieving balance between work responsibilities, personal goals, and rest is a central pillar of emotional self-care. When your schedule leaves no breathing room, your mind has fewer chances to reset, making you prone to mental fatigue and regret.

- **Protected Off-Time**: Schedule a few hours each week where you do not check emails or respond to professional calls. Use this period to rest, pursue leisure, or connect with loved ones. Consistency is the key. Let coworkers or friends know of these times so they do not expect immediate responses.
- **Micro-Breaks**: During the workday, take a quick pause every couple of hours—close your eyes, stretch, or simply stand up. These short breaks can stop stress hormones from building up in your system. Even five minutes can refresh your focus and reduce irritability, which in turn lowers the chance of regretful decisions.
- **Vacation Days**: Not everyone can take long holidays, but even one or two days off to read, explore nature, or visit local spots can be healing. Planned downtime helps clear mental clutter and opens new perspectives on whatever regrets you carry.

Balancing responsibilities with rest is not about laziness. It is about preserving energy and mental clarity for the moments when you need to face hard choices or complicated regrets.

---

3. Emotional Literacy: Recognizing and Naming Feelings

Emotional literacy is the skill of identifying, naming, and understanding your emotions. This might sound basic, but many individuals only use broad labels like "bad mood" or "upset." That lack of precision can keep them from pinpointing specific issues. Learning how to recognize a wide range of emotions—such as disappointment, relief, embarrassment, or longing—helps you address them more effectively.

- **Daily Feeling Check**: Set aside a few minutes to ask yourself, "What am I feeling right now?" Perhaps you are anxious about an upcoming work task, or maybe you are relieved that a conflict got resolved. By labeling emotions regularly, you become more in tune with your mental state.
- **Emotional Vocabulary List**: If you struggle to find the right words, keep a simple list of emotion words. When you sense that "bad mood," consult your list and see which word fits best. This practice might reveal that you

are actually "discouraged" rather than "angry," which changes how you respond.
- **Linking Emotions to Actions**: Notice how specific emotions guide your habits. For instance, frustration might lead you to snap at loved ones, or sadness might cause you to withdraw. Tracking these links helps you catch problem behaviors sooner, so you can switch to healthier reactions.

Boosting emotional literacy is not just for personal insight. It also strengthens communication. When you can explain your feelings more clearly, others can respond with greater understanding, reducing miscommunication that often leads to regrets.

---

4. Healthy Expression of Emotions

People who rarely release their emotions can end up with layers of unspoken regret, anger, or sadness. Properly expressing how you feel helps you stay mentally balanced. It is not just about venting frustrations; it is also about constructive channels for them.

- **Journaling**: Writing down your feelings is a private way to let out tension. This can be a simple notebook or a digital file. Do not worry about perfect grammar or style. The point is to let your thoughts flow without censorship. Over time, you might notice patterns that guide you in reducing triggers for regret.
- **Artistic Outlets**: Activities like painting, sketching, singing, or playing a musical instrument can channel intense emotions when words fail. Art forms a bridge between your internal state and the outside world, offering a safe way to transform raw feelings into something creative.
- **Talk with a Trusted Person**: Discussing your emotional state with a friend, counselor, or family member can release stress. You do not have to solve every problem in these talks—just naming and sharing the emotion can be enough. However, choose your confidant carefully. Not everyone is prepared to respond with empathy.

Consistently engaging in healthy emotional expression keeps negative feelings from lingering. Over time, it also gives you room to handle regret more calmly because you are not weighed down by layers of repressed emotions.

5. Boundary-Setting as Self-Care

Boundaries define what you find acceptable in interactions and what you will not tolerate. Without clear boundaries, you risk letting people drain your emotional energy or push you into situations that lead to regret. Boundary-setting is a form of self-care because it protects your emotional well-being from external demands.

- **Personal Space and Time**: Let others know when you are unavailable for calls, messages, or favors. While it might feel selfish at first, consistent boundary enforcement can reduce regrets about never having personal time.
- **Emotional Boundaries**: If someone's jokes or comments hurt you, speak up. Politely but firmly mention that those words cross a line. Doing so early prevents feelings of lingering resentment and regret for staying silent.
- **Digital Boundaries**: With phones and social media, people can reach you anytime. Consider silencing notifications after a certain hour or uninstalling certain apps for periods of the day. These steps can safeguard your headspace from constant outside pressures.

By setting clear boundaries, you show respect for yourself and teach others to do the same. Strong boundaries create an emotional safety zone where regrets have less power to grow.

---

6. Practical Relaxation Methods

Relaxation is not a luxury; it is a core part of emotional self-care. Chronic tension can heighten regrets, making small problems feel massive. If your mind rarely rests, you cannot process regrets in a balanced manner.

- **Breathing Exercises**: Slow, controlled breathing signals the brain to calm down. For instance, try inhaling for four counts, holding for one count, then exhaling for four counts. Do several rounds when you feel the pressure of regret building.
- **Progressive Muscle Relaxation**: Tense and release muscle groups from head to toe. This technique lowers overall tension and brings your attention back to the body instead of swirling regretful thoughts.

- **Nature Breaks**: Step outside for a few minutes each day. If possible, observe plants or a nearby park. Even limited exposure to natural settings can ease stress chemicals in your body.

These activities, performed consistently, create moments of tranquility. As a result, you approach regret with more composure, rather than being stuck in a loop of dread.

---

7. The Role of Nutrition and Exercise in Emotional Balance

People often overlook the impact of physical health on emotional well-being. Yet, your diet, exercise habits, and sleep patterns significantly affect your mental state. Poor nutrition and inactivity can worsen mood swings, contributing to regretful thinking.

- **Stable Eating Routines**: Aim for balanced meals that provide steady energy. Skipping meals or consuming excessive junk food can spark blood sugar spikes and crashes, leading to irritability. Irritability can trigger rash decisions or harsh self-criticism—common sources of regret.
- **Regular Physical Activity**: Exercise releases endorphins, which improve mood and reduce stress. You do not need extreme workouts; even a 20-minute walk can help. Over time, consistent movement leads to clearer thinking and a calmer reaction to regrets.
- **Adequate Rest**: Lack of sleep weakens emotional control. If you regularly sleep fewer hours than you need, you become prone to overreacting or making unwise choices, heightening the risk of regret. Cultivating a regular sleep schedule is a foundational part of emotional self-care.

Your body and mind are connected. By taking small but steady steps toward better physical health, you build a more stable emotional platform for dealing with regrets.

---

8. Self-Compassion Techniques

Self-compassion is the ability to show kindness and understanding toward yourself, especially in times of difficulty. People with low self-compassion often respond to mistakes with harsh criticism, which inflates regret. Cultivating self-compassion lowers the intensity of negative self-talk.

- **Replace Self-Criticism with Encouragement**: When you find yourself saying, "I messed up again," try to insert a more supportive comment: "Yes, that was a mistake, but I can learn from it." This shift might feel awkward at first, but repeated practice helps it become natural.
- **Mental Image of a Supportive Figure**: Picture someone who cares about you—a parent, a friend, or even a fictional character—comforting you when regret surfaces. Although imaginary, this mental exercise can evoke genuine feelings of safety and remind you that mistakes do not reduce your worth.
- **Forgiveness Exercises**: Write a note to yourself stating what you forgive yourself for. It could be a missed opportunity, a broken promise, or a harsh word said in anger. Include the lessons you learned and express your intent to move forward. Reviewing this note can lower self-blame and pave the way for healthier emotional processing.

Self-compassion does not justify irresponsibility. Instead, it breaks the destructive pattern of self-hate that prevents real solutions and growth.

---

9. Setting Realistic Expectations

Unrealistic expectations are a main contributor to regret. If you aim for absolute perfection in every task, you are almost guaranteed to feel disappointed. Part of emotional self-care involves setting goals that are challenging yet achievable, so you avoid the constant frustration of falling short of impossible standards.

- **SMART Goals**: Specific, Measurable, Achievable, Relevant, and Time-bound. For instance, rather than saying, "I need to be the best employee," say, "I will improve my presentation skills by attending one workshop and practicing public speaking for 10 minutes daily over the next two months."
- **Check-in Points**: Along the way, evaluate whether you are meeting milestones. If you find you aimed too high or too low, adjust. This flexible approach lets you reduce regrets about failing to hit unrealistic targets.
- **Self-Reflection**: Ask yourself if you are using social comparison or illusions to set expectations. If your yardstick for success is another

person's highlight reel, you may be chasing something that is not even real for them. Focus on your authentic goals rather than external benchmarks.

By refining expectations to match real-world situations, you lower the chance of regret when things do not unfold perfectly.

---

10. Social Support as Emotional Self-Care

Emotional self-care does not have to be a solo task. Close relationships can serve as protective buffers, especially when you face regrets. Sharing feelings in a trusted network can relieve mental strain and bring new perspectives.

- **Friends and Family**: Let them know, in general terms, when you are going through a rough time. You do not have to reveal every detail, but a small update can invite their care and empathy. Their words or even their silent presence can be reassuring when regret looms.
- **Support Groups**: If your regrets revolve around a specific issue—like addiction recovery or grief—joining a group of people with similar experiences can be life-changing. Hearing stories of how others overcame regret and seeing that you are not alone can offer a big emotional boost.
- **Professional Guidance**: Sometimes regrets are rooted in deep pain or complicated emotional patterns. Therapists, counselors, or coaches are trained to guide you through those layers. They provide structured methods to address regret, form better coping mechanisms, and plan future improvements.

Social support is not a sign of weakness. It is a recognition that humans thrive in supportive connections. By seeking and giving support, you enrich your emotional self-care environment.

---

11. Using Time Wisely for Emotional Health

Time is a limited resource, and the way we spend it can cause or lessen regret. Procrastination, overcommitting, or poor planning can inflate stress and leave you doubting your choices.

- **Proactive Scheduling**: Each week, list tasks and events in order of importance. Tackle priority items first, so you do not end up in last-minute chaos that fuels regret.
- **Buffer Zones**: Build small gaps between tasks. Leaving 15-minute cushions can prevent the ripple effect of running late. This calm approach helps you handle unexpected changes without panic, reducing mistakes you might regret.
- **Time for Hobbies**: Engaging in activities for enjoyment—not just for productivity—replenishes emotional energy. Hobbies can refresh your mindset and lower the chance of feeling regretful about having no relaxation time. Even 30 minutes a day can make a difference.

Managing your time with your mental health in mind stops regret from piling up due to neglected priorities or too many rushed decisions.

---

12. Self-Care Checkpoints to Monitor Progress

Change happens gradually. Create short self-care "checkpoints" to track how well your efforts are working. Every month or two, ask yourself:

1. **Am I feeling less overwhelmed by regret?**
   If yes, keep doing what works. If no, figure out which area of your routine might need adjusting.
2. **Which emotional self-care methods do I skip most often?**
   Sometimes we avoid the methods we need the most, perhaps because they challenge us.
3. **How is my stress level over time?**
   Tracking your average stress can reveal if you are improving or if new problems are arising that require more attention.
4. **Do I see improvements in my relationships or overall mood?**
   Emotional self-care often leads to a ripple effect. If you notice less conflict or more patience with others, it is a good sign.

These checkpoints help you stay accountable. They also let you fine-tune your strategies before regret grows too large.

---

13. Avoiding Overreliance on Quick Fixes

In modern life, there is a tendency to look for "instant cures"—like binge-watching shows, overeating comfort food, or scrolling social media endlessly. While these activities may distract you from regret briefly, they do not solve the underlying issues. Emotional self-care is about stable, lasting improvement.

- **Mindful Leisure**: If you want to watch a show or play a game, do it consciously. Decide how much time you will spend and avoid letting it consume your day. This mindful approach reduces the guilt or regret that often follows excessive indulgence.
- **Substance Awareness**: Alcohol or other substances can seem to relieve regret for a moment, but they often worsen negative feelings later. Part of emotional self-care involves evaluating if your coping methods cause more harm in the long run.
- **Therapy Instead of Numbing**: If regret is intense, short-term distractions might fail to help. Professional therapy offers a path to face root causes rather than masking pain. It can feel challenging, but it usually leads to deeper relief and personal growth.

Relying on quick fixes might bring regrets about wasted time or harmful side effects. Sustainable emotional self-care aims for steady progress instead of temporary relief followed by deeper regret.

---

14. Handling Setbacks Gracefully

Even with a strong self-care routine, setbacks happen. You might slip up in your new habits or face sudden crises. The key is not to interpret these setbacks as proof of failure, which can fuel regret. Instead, use them as markers to adjust your approach.

- **Resetting Routines**: If you abandon your self-care plan for a few weeks, simply restart. Every day is a new chance to pick up healthy habits again.
- **Learning from the Slip**: Ask yourself what triggered the setback. Did you overcommit at work? Did you have a personal conflict that drained your energy? Identifying triggers can help you prepare next time.

- **Offer Yourself Patience**: Growth is rarely linear. Remind yourself that every step backward can still teach valuable lessons. The difference between falling completely off track and bouncing back often lies in the kindness you show yourself during rough patches.

Viewing setbacks as part of the process reduces the guilt and regret that typically arise when things do not go perfectly. This kinder perspective sustains your emotional self-care over the long term.

---

15. Long-Term Benefits of Emotional Self-Care

When you practice emotional self-care consistently, a few long-term changes become noticeable:

1. **Better Stress Management**: You do not react to problems with panic or anger as often. This steadiness reduces regret caused by rash comments or actions.
2. **Higher Self-Esteem**: As you honor your emotional needs, you affirm your worth. Over time, this builds confidence that lowers chronic self-doubt, which often fuels regret.
3. **Healthier Relationships**: Emotionally balanced people are more patient, understanding, and clear in communication. This healthiness in relationships cuts down on conflicts that lead to regret.
4. **Adaptability**: Challenges will keep coming, but emotional self-care makes you flexible in response. You are less likely to feel trapped by regretful incidents because you have the tools to handle them.

These outcomes reflect a shift in how you see yourself and the world. Instead of fearing regret, you trust in your resilience. That trust grows each time you face difficulties yet remain centered through ongoing emotional self-care.

---

16. Putting Emotional Self-Care into Action

To integrate these ideas into everyday life, consider the following:

- **Plan It**: Choose a realistic schedule for self-care. Maybe 10 minutes every morning for meditation, plus 30 minutes of exercise on weekends, plus a weekly chat with a close friend.
- **Keep It Simple**: Do not aim for extreme routines right away. Gradual changes are more likely to stick. A 5-minute breathing exercise is better than zero, especially if done regularly.
- **Track Your Mood**: Notice how you feel before and after a self-care activity. Over a few weeks, look for patterns. Maybe yoga helps a lot, or maybe journaling suits you best.
- **Adjust as Needed**: Life situations change. If you find journaling gets boring, try an art-related approach. If your schedule shifts, find new time slots. Adapting keeps self-care relevant instead of letting it fade.

Emotional self-care is a personal, evolving practice. There is no single formula for everyone. The crucial factor is consistency—making sure you frequently check in with your feelings and actively support yourself.

---

17. Final Thoughts on Emotional Self-Care

Regret can become a heavy presence if you lack daily emotional nourishment. By focusing on balanced work-rest patterns, healthy emotional expression, constructive boundaries, and realistic expectations, you secure a sturdier mental foundation. This foundation acts as a buffer against future regrets and provides the calm needed to address old ones in a healthier way.

Even if your past regrets are profound, emotional self-care offers a path to soften their sting. It allows you to face mistakes with clarity and self-compassion, reducing self-punishment and guiding you toward solutions. The more you honor your emotional needs, the less control regret holds over you. This resilience carries forward as you continue exploring new ways to manage regret, build better habits, and move toward a life with more inner peace.

CHAPTER 14: TRANSFORMING REGRET INTO CONSTRUCTIVE INSIGHTS

Regret carries the painful memory of past decisions, but it also holds clues that can lead to significant personal improvements. The challenge is learning how to convert regret from mere sadness or guilt into something that drives you to take smarter steps. In this chapter, we explore methods for turning regret into practical wisdom that helps you refine your future actions. By applying reflection, careful planning, and a willingness to experiment, you can pull valuable lessons out of your regrets and ensure they serve a positive purpose.

1. The Value of Looking at Regret as Data

Instead of seeing regret solely as an emotional burden, try to view it as information. Each regretful event reveals something about your choices, your assumptions, or the context in which you acted. For example, if you regret quitting a job hastily, that might highlight a tendency to make big decisions under emotional strain. Or if you regret a financial deal that went wrong, it might show a gap in your research process.

Treating regret as data means you investigate each regret with curiosity. You ask: "What does this event tell me about my decision-making style, my values, or the skills I lack?" This new perspective prevents regrets from staying stuck as pure self-criticism. Instead, you shift to a problem-solving mindset where regret points you toward areas to strengthen.

2. Structured Reflection: The "Post-Event Review"

Businesses and sports teams often do a "post-event review" to evaluate performance. You can borrow the same method for your personal regrets:

1. **Describe the Regret**: Summarize what happened. Was it a project that failed, an exam you did not prepare for, or a relationship that ended?
2. **Identify Main Factors**: List any conditions that contributed—time constraints, misinformation, or emotional states.

3. **Check Your Input**: Examine how your actions or inactions shaped the result. Maybe you acted impulsively or did not gather enough facts.
4. **Brainstorm Alternative Approaches**: Think about what you could have done differently if you had known then what you know now.
5. **Outline Lessons**: Write down what stands out as the main takeaway. This is where regret transitions to insight.

Keep your notes in a place you can revisit. When a similar decision pops up, review your previous post-event reviews to prevent repeating the same mistakes.

---

3. Looking for Patterns Across Multiple Regrets

Sometimes one regret does not reveal a full pattern, but several regrets together might. For instance, if you notice you have financial regrets tied to impulse buying, you can see a pattern of poor planning around money. Or if relationship regrets often involve neglecting communication, that might be an ongoing skill gap. Spotting patterns helps you address root causes rather than fixing each regret in isolation.

- **Create a Regret Timeline**: Write down major regrets in chronological order. Note your personal state at the time, who was around you, and what your main motivators were. Any recurring theme stands out more on a timeline.
- **Root Cause Analysis**: Ask "why" multiple times. For example, "Why did I quit my job too soon? Because I was unhappy daily. Why was I unhappy? Because I did not speak up about changes I needed. Why did I not speak up? Because I feared rejection." This chain reveals a deeper cause—fear of rejection—that might appear in other regrets as well.

Recognizing these threads helps you develop broad solutions. In the example above, learning assertiveness might fix multiple regret patterns at once.

---

4. Building New Skills Based on Regret Insights

Regret frequently highlights areas of personal or professional development that need attention. For example, if you regret failing a presentation, you might enroll in a public speaking course. If you regret a missed opportunity in networking, you could start practicing small talk or join a local professional group. Each regret can point directly to a skill you can learn.

- **Identify the Skills**: After each regret, note which skill could have helped you avoid or fix the issue. It might be time management, negotiation, emotional regulation, or technical knowledge.
- **Pick One to Focus on**: Trying to fix everything at once can be overwhelming. Choose the most relevant skill to tackle first. You can always move on to others as you see progress.
- **Use the Lesson as Motivation**: Every time you feel unmotivated to learn the new skill, remember how regret feels. This memory can fuel your determination and keep you on track.

Turning regret into a trigger for skill-building ensures that you do not repeat the same mistakes. It also boosts your self-confidence because you see that regrets can be catalysts for personal improvement rather than stagnant sorrow.

---

5. Gentle Self-Inquiry Instead of Blame

When using regret to gain insights, watch out for the trap of self-blame. Blame turns your attention to guilt, while inquiry looks for understanding. One way to do this is:

- **Use Neutral Language**: Instead of saying, "I was so stupid to trust that person," say, "I placed trust in that person, and the result was negative. Let me explore why I trusted them without double-checking." This neutral phrasing encourages learning rather than self-attack.
- **Stay in the Present**: Avoid language like, "I should have known better," because it assumes you had the same knowledge then that you do now. Instead, say, "Back then, I did not have all the details. Next time, I will gather more background before committing."

- **Imagine Advising a Friend**: If you feel stuck in blame, pretend a close friend is telling you about the same regret. How would you respond? You would likely show understanding and help them see ways to grow.

This style of inquiry helps you remain calm and rational, which is vital for drawing constructive insights from regret. Blame only adds emotional weight without offering solutions.

---

6. Testing New Behaviors in Real Situations

Insights from regret remain theory unless you practice them in actual scenarios. For instance, if your regret taught you that you need better boundaries with coworkers, try a small step the next time your coworker asks for help during your lunch break. Politely explain that you need to protect your break time. Observe the outcome. Did it lessen your stress? Do you feel less regret about how your day went?

- **Plan the Small Change**: Be very specific about what new behavior you will apply and when.
- **Implement and Observe**: Carry out the plan, pay attention to your feelings, and see if it aligns with the lessons from your regret.
- **Adjust If Needed**: If the new approach creates new problems, refine it. For example, maybe you need a balanced approach—agree to help occasionally, but only when your own tasks are not pressing.

Making small but real-life modifications keeps the lessons from regret active, preventing them from slipping back into mere wishes.

---

7. Harnessing Regret to Challenge Mindsets

Some regrets might point to flawed mindsets, like a "fixed mindset" that sees abilities as unchangeable. If, for instance, you regret not applying for a job because you assumed you would fail, that regret indicates a limiting belief. By facing it, you notice how your mindset blocked growth. This awareness can lead you to adopt a "growth mindset," believing you can improve with effort.

- **Rewrite Limiting Beliefs**: If you identify the belief "I'm not good at learning new skills," rephrase it as "I can get better through focused effort and the right methods."
- **Collect Evidence of Growth**: Each time you improve even slightly, note it. If you used to be poor at public speaking but now can handle small team talks, that is proof that change is possible.
- **Watch Negative Self-Talk**: Mindsets often show up as internal remarks like, "I can't do this." Counter them with facts—past examples of progress, examples of others who learned the same skill, or logical reasoning.

Challenging rigid mindsets helps you go beyond regret and seize future opportunities, so you do not repeat the same missed chances again.

---

8. Emotional Release Alongside Analysis

Transforming regret into insights does not mean ignoring the emotional aspect. Sometimes you need a good cry or a serious talk with a friend about the pain of the past event. Emotional release is part of fully processing regret. After you release those feelings, you often have clearer mental space to examine lessons.

- **Rituals for Letting Go**: Some people find it helpful to write the regret on a piece of paper, tear it up, and throw it away. Others might say a silent acknowledgment like, "I release you, regret. Thank you for teaching me." While symbolic, these acts can provide emotional closure, making it easier to move into a rational analysis.
- **Combining Therapy and Action**: If regret is tied to deep trauma or long-term issues, therapy can guide you to handle the emotional layers. In parallel, you can keep a practical journal to track the steps you are taking to avoid repeating the regretful pattern.

A balanced approach of emotional acceptance plus solution-oriented thinking ensures that regret does not trap you in sorrow. Instead, it moves you forward with a deeper understanding of what you need.

---

9. Communicating Regret to Others for Shared Growth

Some regrets involve other people—friends, family, colleagues. Sharing your insights with them can help everyone learn. For instance, if you regret how you handled a group project, you might talk about it openly at the next team meeting, acknowledging your part and suggesting new methods.

- **Take Responsibility**: Communicate that you see your role in the problem. This honesty can motivate others to be transparent about their roles too.
- **Focus on Forward Action**: Express that your main reason for bringing it up is to propose better approaches in the future. This keeps the conversation constructive rather than blaming.
- **Encourage Input**: Ask for suggestions from others. Regret can be a group learning opportunity when everyone is invited to share perspectives and solutions.

Sharing regret-driven insights fosters an atmosphere of honest growth. You not only transform your own regrets but also help your community or workplace avoid repeated mistakes.

---

10. Gratitude for Lessons Learned

While it may feel strange to link regret with gratitude, the two can coexist. When you notice how regretful moments led you to change for the better, gratitude can arise. For instance, you might regret not paying enough attention to your health until you had a scare, yet you feel grateful that this wake-up call spurred you to adopt healthier habits.

- **Reflect on Gains**: List ways your regretful experiences made you more empathetic, careful, or skilled. This does not minimize the pain but recognizes that positives can emerge.
- **Pair Regret with Thanks**: Each time regret returns, you can remind yourself, "This regret was hard, but it taught me [specific lesson]. I'm thankful for that growth."
- **Mental Shift**: Over time, your regret might become less about shame and more about how it shaped your future path. This shift can release you from harsh self-judgment.

Gratitude does not mean you are happy about mistakes. It means you appreciate the insight gained, which helps you accept the past and invest in better outcomes moving forward.

11. Setting a Regret-Review Schedule

To keep regret-based insights fresh, try scheduling a regular "regret review." This does not mean wallowing in sadness. Instead, it is a systematic check on whether you are applying the lessons.

- **Monthly or Quarterly Check**: Pick a day to sit with your regret journal or mental notes. Look at the regrets you have analyzed, see how well you have applied the insights, and note any progress or new challenges.
- **Highlight Achievements**: Celebrate small victories—like remembering not to use the disallowed word for "celebrate," so here we might say "recognize successes." If you overcame a pattern that once caused regret, acknowledge that milestone.
- **Plan Next Steps**: If you find a lesson is still unaddressed, make a specific plan for the coming period. Perhaps you will take a workshop or practice a new skill. This consistent attention helps you keep regret from fading into the background without truly learning from it.

Such a routine prevents regrets from piling up. You maintain a proactive stance, ensuring that each regret is fully transformed into a stepping stone rather than a constant source of remorse.

12. Creating Future Safeguards

Once you have gleaned insights from a regret, it is wise to embed safeguards so you will not forget. For example:

- **Decision Rules**: If you learned to avoid signing contracts without reading the fine print, create a personal rule: "I never sign anything important on the same day I receive it." This rule acts as a buffer against impulsive actions.

- **Advice Network**: If you regret ignoring outside opinions, designate a few people you trust and vow to consult them before big moves. Over time, they become your safety net.
- **Reminders and Prompts**: Use phone alarms or sticky notes to remind you of critical lessons, such as "Take a breath before responding to conflict." This small prompt can prevent you from repeating impulsive errors.

Safeguards transform insights into regular habits, lowering the chance that you will slip back into the same behaviors that led to regret.

---

13. Shifting from Punishment to Growth

Some people feel the need to punish themselves for regrets, as though suffering will balance the mistake. This can lead to damaging cycles of self-denial or sabotaging new opportunities. A more productive approach is to see mistakes as part of growth. The aim is not to punish yourself but to make sure you truly learn and apply lessons.

- **Self-Forgiveness Statements**: Calmly say to yourself, "I acknowledge I made a mistake. I will repay this mistake with sincere improvement rather than constant self-blame."
- **Helping Others**: If your regret involved harming someone else, you can make amends by apologizing or doing something beneficial for them if possible. Channeling your remorse into helpful actions fosters growth instead of guilt.
- **Value-Focused Living**: Remind yourself of your key values—honesty, compassion, responsibility. Each time you act in alignment with these values, you are healing the regrets of past misalignment. This slow but steady shift cements your new direction.

By moving from punishment to growth, regret becomes a motivator for positive change rather than a permanent emotional prison.

---

14. Combining Regret Insights with Future Dreams

Regret often shows you what you do not want. Future dreams illustrate what you do want. Weave these together for a clearer roadmap. For example, if you regret spending years in a job you hated, and you dream of launching your own business, use that regret to power your planning. Remembering how it felt to be stuck can push you to plan finances, network, and skill up carefully to follow your goal.

- **Create a Vision Board**: Include pictures or keywords that represent your hopes. Also add small references to your regrets as reminders of what to avoid.
- **Inverse Planning**: Sometimes you can define your future path by identifying what you want to steer clear of. If a specific regret was about neglecting family, you might schedule weekly family dinners or free weekends to ensure you do not repeat the same mistake.
- **Motivation from Contrast**: Each step toward your dream can feel more meaningful when you remember what regret taught you. This contrast motivates you to keep going, especially when obstacles arise.

Blending regret's lessons with future dreams helps you avoid drifting. You move with intention, guided by both your past experiences and your aspirations.

---

15. Teaching What You Have Learned

Sharing what you have gleaned from regret can enhance your own learning. Teaching is a powerful reinforcement tool. It pushes you to articulate ideas clearly and spot any gaps in your understanding.

- **Casual Mentoring**: If you have a friend or colleague facing a similar risk, gently share your story and how you navigated regret. Remember to maintain respect for their autonomy.
- **Online Platforms**: Writing a short article or social media post about what you learned from a regret can reach many people. Their questions or comments might deepen your insight.
- **Community Workshops**: If you are comfortable, you might host small workshops (even virtually) to discuss common regrets in your field—such

as financial mistakes or career missteps—and propose preventive measures.

By teaching, you refine your own lessons. You also shift the narrative around regret: it stops being a shameful secret and becomes a collective resource that can guide others.

---

16. Keeping Hope Alive

When regrets pile up, hope can fade. You might think, "I keep failing. Maybe it will never change." That mindset blocks the transformation of regret into constructive insight. Maintaining hope is essential because it fuels the effort needed to apply lessons.

- **Highlight Every Improvement**: Even if your overall situation remains tough, note small signs of progress. For instance, "I lost my temper fewer times this week compared to last week."
- **Remember Past Victories**: List times you overcame past challenges. This serves as proof that you are capable of growth. It reminds you that regrets have not stopped you before and do not have to stop you now.
- **Seek Positive Role Models**: Look for individuals who have turned their mistakes around. Their stories confirm that regret does not define your future. If possible, connect with them or read about their experiences to glean practical tips on maintaining hope.

Hope is not blind optimism. It is faith in your ability to learn and adapt. Without it, regret can become a permanent drain. With hope, each regret is a stepping stone to something better.

---

17. Long-Term Mindset: Continuous Self-Revision

Transforming regret into insights is not a one-time fix. Life keeps evolving, and new regrets may emerge. The best approach is a mindset of continuous self-revision. You accept that you are always a work in progress. Each mistake or shortfall adds depth to your understanding.

- **Frequent Self-Audits**: Periodically ask: "Am I still applying the key lessons from past regrets? Are there new regrets forming?" This keeps you active in self-improvement.
- **Adapt to New Stages**: As you shift careers, enter new relationships, or move to different life phases, old lessons might need updates. For example, time management lessons from your early career might need rethinking in parenthood or retirement.
- **Celebrate Gains**: Recognize your achievements along the path. You have come a long way from where you started. Noting that growth fuels further progress.

Through continuous self-revision, regret remains a source of ongoing enrichment instead of a final verdict on your worth. Each insight refines your behavior, your mindset, and your life's direction.

---

18. Conclusion of Chapter 14

Turning regret into constructive insight is a skill that takes reflection, willingness to learn, and steady action. Rather than leaving regret as a painful memory, you dissect it to expose lessons about your choices, habits, or mindset. You apply those lessons in real life, test new behaviors, and form personal safeguards so you do not repeat the same errors.

This transformation demands a balanced approach. You must allow yourself to feel the emotional weight, yet also shift into problem-solving mode. Along the way, self-forgiveness and hope keep you from getting stuck in blame. Over time, regrets once seen as burdens can become catalysts for remarkable personal growth, shaping wiser decisions and richer relationships. By viewing your regrets as teachers, you ensure that your past missteps fuel a better future rather than holding you back.

CHAPTER 15: REPAIRING PERSONAL RELATIONSHIPS

Regret can be heavy when it involves people we care about. Sometimes, we look back on words we spoke in anger, mistakes that shattered trust, or missed moments we can never get back. While some relationships may fade permanently, many can still be healed to some degree if we take deliberate steps. This chapter looks at practical methods to fix damaged bonds, offer genuine apologies, and build a healthier connection going forward. We will consider the many obstacles that can arise—pride, fear, misunderstanding—and discover ways to address them so regret about lost or weakened relationships does not stay a permanent wound.

---

1. Why Relationship-Based Regret Hurts So Deeply

Regret tied to relationships cuts to our core because people matter profoundly in our lives. Whether it is a friend, spouse, family member, or even a coworker, relationships shape our emotions and sense of belonging. When we hurt someone or drift apart, the loss is not just about the event but about the warmth and support we once shared. Humans thrive on connection, so damaging a meaningful tie often leads to a mix of sadness, guilt, and longing.

Additionally, broken relationships can disturb our self-image. We might see ourselves as caring, honest, or loving, yet a major conflict or mistake contradicts that view. This creates an internal clash: we wonder if we truly are the person we believed ourselves to be. It is this combination of sorrow and identity threat that makes relationship regrets especially intense.

---

2. Facing Your Part in the Conflict

Reconciliation starts with owning your role in what went wrong. This can be difficult if you believe the other person is mostly at fault. However, focusing only on what the other party did can prevent positive change. A more constructive approach is to isolate your own actions or words that contributed. Even if those actions are smaller than what the other person did, acknowledging them is a sign of responsibility.

- **Identify Your Missteps**: Think about the exact phrases you used, the times you failed to show empathy, or the way you broke trust. Write them down in simple terms without making excuses. If you feel defensive, note that too, but keep your focus on what you could have handled differently.
- **Separate Intent from Impact**: You might not have intended to harm the other person, but the effect was still pain or distance. Recognizing the gap between your intention and their experience shows you are trying to see things from their perspective.
- **Avoid Self-Flagellation**: Accepting your part does not mean calling yourself worthless. Instead of thinking, "I am a terrible individual," say, "I made these mistakes, and I can change."

This step is necessary because attempts to fix a relationship fall short if you do not accept your portion of the blame. When you demonstrate true ownership of your actions, it becomes easier for the other person to consider the chance of re-engaging with you.

---

3. The Power of a Genuine Apology

Apologies are a key tool for repairing damage, but they only work if they are sincere and thorough. A hollow or vague apology ("I'm sorry if you were hurt") often worsens resentment. A deeper apology includes several elements:

1. **Acknowledgment of Harm**: Specify what you did and how it affected the other person. For example, "I realize my harsh words made you feel humiliated in front of others."
2. **Taking Responsibility**: State that you alone are responsible for your own actions. Do not blame circumstances or the other person for your choices.
3. **Expression of Regret**: Show that you honestly wish things had gone differently. Avoid minimizing the hurt. Instead, let them know you fully grasp the seriousness of the issue.
4. **Willingness to Listen**: Let the other person speak about how they feel. An apology is not just about your words; it is also about hearing their perspective and giving them space to express any lingering hurt.

5. **Plan for Change**: Propose how you will handle similar situations in the future. If you often spoke rudely, you might mention steps you will take—like pausing before responding in conflict, or seeking communication coaching.

When done with patience and clarity, an apology can soften the tension and rebuild a foundation of trust. The other person sees your regret is real and that you respect their feelings enough to name your wrongdoing directly.

---

4. Letting the Other Person Have Time

Even the best apology cannot force immediate forgiveness. Emotional wounds may be fresh, or they might have accumulated over years. Pushing the other person to accept your remorse right away can be counterproductive, as it may seem like you are more focused on relieving your guilt than attending to their pain. Instead, let them process it on their own schedule.

- **Send a Thoughtful Message**: If direct conversation is not possible, you might write a carefully worded letter that shows you understand the harm done. Then give them space.
- **Respect Boundaries**: If they say they need a few weeks or even months before talking about it again, respect that limit. Pressuring them might reopen the wound.
- **Gentle Check-Ins**: After a while, a brief message or note that says, "I'm still here and open to talk if you want" can be helpful. This is not demanding; it is simply letting them know you remain available.

This space can feel painful because you want resolution. But rushing may only deepen regret if the other person feels coerced. Allow the relationship time to breathe while keeping communication lines open in a calm, respectful way.

---

5. Managing Mixed Feelings: Love and Anger Together

Sometimes, relationship regret is complicated by conflicting feelings. You might still love the person but feel angry about how they responded. Or you may want to fix the bond but also carry fear they could hurt you again. These mixed emotions can slow or derail the reconciliation process.

- **Self-Check**: Recognize that multiple emotions can coexist. Write them out: "I love them, I'm mad at them, I miss them, I'm scared." Identifying your emotional landscape prevents confusion from bottling it all up.
- **Look at the Source of Anger**: Are you angry because they did not meet your expectation, or because you are upset at yourself for letting a situation continue? Sorting out the root can help you address the right issue, whether it is boundary-setting or rethinking your own approach.
- **Consider a Mediator**: If the relationship is high-stakes—a close family bond or a long-term friendship—you could invite a neutral party (a counselor or a trusted mutual friend) to help navigate conversations. They can keep discussions fair and ensure that both sides feel heard.

Mixed feelings do not mean the relationship is beyond repair. They are simply a sign that human connections are rarely black-and-white. You can hold more than one emotion at a time and still move forward if you address each part honestly.

---

6. Rebuilding Trust Step by Step

One of the biggest regrets in relationships involves broken trust—perhaps through dishonesty, betrayal, or repeated letdowns. Re-earning trust is difficult because trust forms gradually through consistent evidence of reliability. A single promise or apology is rarely enough.

- **Consistency is Key**: If you pledge to change a habit, follow through every day. This reliability, over weeks and months, can gradually melt the other person's doubts.
- **Transparency**: Where possible, let them see you are genuine. For instance, if the conflict was about finances, you might volunteer to show your budget records so they feel reassured.
- **Meeting Small Needs**: Sometimes big gestures are less convincing than steady support in daily life. Showing up on time, sending a supportive message, or offering to help with tasks can speak volumes about your changed attitude.

- **Recognize Incremental Gains**: If you see the other person beginning to trust you for small things, recognize this moment. It might be the first sign that the bond is healing. A small "thank you for trusting me today" can encourage them to keep opening up.

Rebuilding trust can be lengthy, but do not get discouraged if progress is slow. Consistency and patience often matter more than dramatic apologies.

---

7. Understanding Relationship "Cycles"

Some relationships follow repeated patterns—fights, short-lived peace, then fights again. If regret stems from such cycles, it is important to spot the triggers and typical sequence. For example, a couple might always argue about finances when bills are due, or siblings might fight whenever a certain relative visits. Knowing the cycle helps you step in earlier and handle the situation differently.

- **Document the Cycle**: Sketch out how each conflict tends to start, escalate, and resolve. Identify your role in each stage.
- **Plan Interruptions**: Once you see the pattern, decide on a small change that can break it. If you argue under stress at the end of the week, plan a calm conversation earlier in the week to address concerns.
- **Preventive Communication**: If you notice tension building, speak up gently before the typical blowout happens. This can feel odd at first, but it might stop the old cycle from repeating and leaving you with the same regret again.

Acknowledging the repetitive nature of conflicts can free you from blaming everything on one event. Instead, you can adopt a problem-solving attitude about the repeated dynamic that leads to regret.

---

8. Using Regret to Understand Deeper Needs

Sometimes, regret emerges because we realize we lacked empathy, patience, or quality time with the other person. This signals an unmet need in the relationship—either for them, for you, or both. Examining regret can highlight these deeper requirements.

- **Ask What Was Missing**: Did the other person feel unappreciated? Did you feel unheard? Pinpointing these needs is essential to avoid repeating the same mistakes.
- **Negotiate New Approaches**: If the root issue was lack of time spent together, brainstorm ways to include regular shared activities or simpler check-ins. If the need was emotional support, consider scheduling short daily talks about each other's day.
- **Respect Individual Differences**: People have diverse ways of feeling valued—some need verbal affirmations, others need small gestures. Understanding each other's preference can prevent accidental hurt or neglect.

Regret then becomes a prompt for better alignment. You recognize that the conflict showed a gap in how you meet each other's needs. By identifying and working on that gap, you strengthen the relationship beyond just fixing the immediate regret.

---

9. Setting Realistic Expectations for the Relationship

Sometimes regret stems from expecting perfection in how others treat us. We might feel let down when reality does not match our ideal. Alternatively, we may over-promise and fail to deliver because the expectations were too high. Setting realistic standards can remove some of the friction that fuels regret.

- **Shared Goal-Setting**: If this is a close relationship, sit down and clarify what each person wants from the bond. Is it daily contact, emotional support, or a sense of independence? Aligning these wants can prevent misunderstandings.
- **Address External Stressors**: Work hours, health problems, and other life factors might limit how much time or energy you can invest. Acknowledge these factors so that no one feels misled.
- **Accept Human Limits**: Everyone has flaws and off days. If you allow space for normal lapses, it is less likely you will blame yourself or the other person for occasional stumbles. This acceptance reduces regret about minor slip-ups.

Realistic expectations do not mean you settle for neglect or harm. They mean you let relationships evolve in a balanced way, without punishing each other for not fulfilling impossible ideals.

---

10. When to Seek Professional Help

Sometimes, the damage is deep, or the patterns are deeply ingrained—such as longstanding resentment in a marriage or repeated betrayals in a family. In such cases, professional counseling can be far more effective than trying to handle it alone. Trained counselors or therapists offer structured methods for dealing with conflict, building empathy, and unpacking deep-seated issues.

- **Individual vs. Group Sessions**: If the other person is willing, going together can help. If not, even solo therapy can guide you to process regret and handle interactions with new strategies.
- **Conflict Resolution Techniques**: Professionals can teach you ways to calm heated exchanges, express emotions more productively, and negotiate solutions. These methods go beyond casual advice, because they are backed by research and guided practice.
- **Neutral Mediation**: Sometimes, families or couples benefit from a mediator who remains fair to both sides. This approach can keep the conversation balanced when one or both parties are upset.

It might feel intimidating to involve a third party, but many people find that without professional help, old regrets keep resurfacing. A therapist can help break those cycles and lay a new foundation for trust.

---

11. Balancing Forgiveness and Self-Protection

Forgiving someone who hurt you (or seeking their forgiveness) does not mean letting your guard down entirely if the behavior might repeat. If the other person's actions were abusive or manipulative, you can accept your regrets about the relationship's breakdown without putting yourself at risk again.

- **Partial Reconciliation**: You might realize that a full restoration is unwise. Instead, you can aim for a civil, respectful dynamic if total closeness is not possible.
- **Clear Boundaries**: If the person's pattern of harming you continues, you can keep physical or emotional distance while still acknowledging the regret over how things turned out. This is a balanced way to protect yourself.
- **Emotional Release**: Forgiveness is more about releasing bitterness than granting permission for the other person to continue their hurtful behavior. You can let go of resentment for your own well-being while staying alert and cautious.

This dual approach allows you to address regret about the relationship while avoiding new harm. It recognizes that not every bond can or should return to what it was, but you can still find closure in how you handle it.

12. Communication Techniques to Prevent Future Regrets

Even after repairing a relationship, new conflicts will appear. To prevent fresh regret, sharpen your communication skills:

- **Active Listening**: Focus on what the other person is saying instead of planning your response. Show you are listening with small nods or short confirmations. This can reduce misunderstandings.
- **Use "I" Statements**: Rather than accusing with "You always do this," say, "I feel upset when this happens because…" This approach lowers defensiveness and fosters constructive dialogue.
- **Timing Matters**: Avoid serious talks when either side is exhausted or rushed. Plan a specific time when both are calm. This approach lessens the chance of regretful words spoken in haste.
- **Clarify Meanings**: If you are unsure what the other person means, ask for details. Often regrets arise from assumptions. A simple question—"Can you explain that further?"—might clear confusion before it escalates.

Proactive communication is like routine maintenance for relationships. It does not remove the possibility of conflict but reduces the chance that minor issues will become major regrets.

13. Self-Forgiveness in the Context of Relationships

When a relationship sours, you might carry regret for years. Even if the other person forgives you, you might struggle to forgive yourself. This self-blame can continue eating at you and might spoil attempts at future connections. Breaking this cycle requires honest acceptance of your past mistakes along with self-compassion.

- **Acceptance of Imperfection**: No one is a flawless partner or friend. Acknowledge that you made poor choices, but do not forget the rest of your qualities. Holding onto the label "bad person" blocks growth.
- **Internal Dialogue**: When regret resurfaces, calmly tell yourself: "I have learned from that event. I am allowed to move forward." Repetition of such affirming thoughts can interrupt negative mental loops.
- **Giving Back**: Sometimes, channeling your regret into positive actions for others can lift the weight of self-blame. For instance, if you regret neglecting an older parent, you might volunteer at a senior center or consistently check on another family member. This does not erase the past but converts remorse into a beneficial act.

Self-forgiveness is not instant, but it is vital. It allows you to re-engage in relationships without the constant fear of repeating the same error. It also fosters a healthier sense of self-worth.

---

14. Recognizing When a Relationship Is Beyond Repair

There are instances where no matter how much you regret and apologize, the other person refuses to meet you halfway. Or the harm done may be so severe that trying to rekindle the relationship only causes more harm. Accepting this truth can be heart-wrenching, but it may be necessary for long-term well-being.

- **Consistent Refusal**: If the other person will not communicate or has explicitly said they want no connection, repeated attempts might only cause them distress and increase your frustration.
- **Ongoing Harm**: If a relationship remains toxic or abusive, chasing reconciliation might trap you in continued harm. Sometimes regret is about letting go for your own safety.

- **Acknowledging Limits**: This does not mean your regret is meaningless. It simply means you have done all you reasonably can, and the outcome is still not what you hoped for. Acceptance of a limit can provide a sort of closure.

Letting go is painful, especially when you truly wanted to fix things. But acknowledging that not every bond can be restored can spare you ongoing guilt and frustration. You can still hold onto the lessons about how to treat others better in the future.

15. Reestablishing Connection through Shared Experiences

If the other person is open to rebuilding the bond, shared positive experiences can mend old wounds in a natural way. Rather than talking endlessly about the past, you can create new memories that breathe fresh air into the relationship.

- **Casual Outings**: A simple meal, a walk in the park, or a coffee break can be easier than a formal sit-down. This relaxed setting helps both sides reconnect without the pressure of a major conversation.
- **Cooperative Tasks**: Doing a project together—like cooking a meal or volunteering—can rebuild teamwork and trust. Actions speak louder than words in showing that you can cooperate again.
- **Reflecting on Progress**: After a few of these shared moments, you might discuss how you both feel about the current state of the relationship. Observing improvements can encourage more steps forward.

These fresh experiences should not be a smokescreen to avoid deeper issues. However, once the big apologies and clarifications have happened, it is often the simple, positive interactions that truly move the relationship past regret.

16. Taking Responsibility for Your Happiness

One potential trap is expecting the other person to fix your sense of well-being. Even if they accept your apology or you both find a new understanding, you might still feel regret if you rely on their constant reassurance. A healthier approach is to find personal fulfillment within yourself. This means pursuing your interests, practicing emotional self-care, and building self-respect so you do not place all emotional weight on the relationship's outcome.

- **Independent Activities**: Maintain some hobbies or friendships that are separate from the repaired relationship. This prevents you from leaning too heavily on that one person.
- **Keep Your Promises to Yourself**: If you pledged to change a habit because it affected the relationship, do it for your own growth as much as for them. That internal motivation is more lasting.
- **Maintain Realistic Hopes**: Even if you reconcile, the relationship might look different than before. By investing in your own sense of purpose and worth, you can handle changes in the dynamic without feeling constant regret or insecurity.

When both parties take charge of their individual happiness, the relationship is more likely to grow on stable ground rather than be a source of repeated regrets.

---

17. Learning from Repaired Bonds

Each repaired relationship offers a blueprint for handling future conflicts better. If you successfully overcame a past misunderstanding, you can apply the same steps—active listening, clear apologies, boundary-setting—to other areas of life. You become more confident that even big missteps can be fixed if handled with honesty and respect.

- **Document the Steps**: If you found certain strategies especially helpful, jot them down. For example, "Having a calm talk after a cooling-off period was far more effective than talking when angry."
- **Spread the Knowledge**: If a friend or colleague confides in you about a damaged relationship, share your insights. While every situation is unique, your story might encourage them to address their conflict calmly instead of letting regret fester.
- **Acknowledge Growth**: Recognize how far you have come since the conflict began. Instead of holding onto the guilt, see the reconciliation as proof that regret can lead to better communication and deeper understanding.

Carrying these lessons forward solidifies the gains you made. It also lessens the fear that you will repeat the same mistakes, thereby lowering future regrets.

18. Conclusion of Chapter 15

Repairing personal relationships after regret can be challenging, but it is often possible through honest admission of wrongdoing, patient apologies, and consistent effort to rebuild trust. Key elements include recognizing your own role, providing a sincere apology, and giving the other person space to process. You can further deepen reconciliation by understanding repeated patterns, clarifying each other's needs, and setting realistic expectations for how the relationship should function.

Sometimes, professional help is essential when wounds are deep or communication is locked in destructive cycles. Forgiveness—whether from the other person or from yourself—does not mean naively forgetting boundaries. Rather, it means letting go of unnecessary resentment while staying thoughtful about protecting each party's well-being.

Ultimately, mending a damaged relationship is a test of patience, empathy, and your willingness to change old habits. Not every bond can be fully restored, and accepting that limit can also release you from some regrets. Yet, when genuine care remains on both sides, even a deeply strained tie can often evolve into a stronger, more respectful connection. Through this journey of reconciliation, regret transforms from a source of pain into a motivation for honest self-improvement and more meaningful bonds.

CHAPTER 16: MANAGING LINGERING SHAME

Regret can come with many emotions—sadness, disappointment, anger—but one of the heaviest is shame. Shame is a powerful feeling that can shape how you see yourself at the deepest level. It can remain even after you have made amends or changed your behavior. In this chapter, we will explore why shame sticks around, how it differs from guilt, and what strategies can help you release that burden. Whether your shame is tied to a minor mistake or a profound lapse in judgment, there are ways to move forward with more self-respect and less constant self-reproach.

---

1. Understanding Shame vs. Guilt

Guilt and shame are related but distinct. Guilt is usually about actions—"I did something wrong." Shame, however, focuses on identity—"I am flawed at my core." When guilt is healthy, it can prompt you to correct a mistake. But shame tends to be deeper and more destructive. It can linger long after the event is done because it is embedded in your self-image.

For instance, if you said harsh words to a friend, guilt might lead you to apologize. If shame is involved, you might think, "I am a horrible person who never deserves real friends." This kind of harsh self-labeling can block progress, feed secrecy, and fuel more regretful behavior. Therefore, shifting from shame to guilt can be a step toward healing, because guilt is more about specific actions that can be changed or atoned for.

---

2. Sources of Lingering Shame

Shame can arise from many places. It might start in childhood if adults or peers criticized you in a personal way—calling you "useless" or "a bad kid" instead of focusing on actions. In adulthood, certain mistakes can trigger shame if you believe they reveal a core defect. Trauma such as abuse or neglect can also plant deep shame, leading you to assume you are unworthy of kindness or success.

- **Cultural or Community Norms**: If your community has strict rules about what is "proper," violating those norms can create shame. Even if you no longer agree with those standards, the emotional imprint can remain.
- **Comparison and Perfectionism**: Seeing others who seem "better" can feed shame, as you feel you do not measure up. This is especially strong on social media, where the highlight reels of others make you believe you are deeply flawed.
- **Internalized Critiques**: Comments from others—like teachers or partners—may stick in your mind, forming an internal critic that repeats negative judgments. Over time, this self-critic is so ingrained that you think it is the truth.

Recognizing the root of shame is important. Shame does not appear out of thin air; it often grows from experiences that taught you to see yourself as defective. Once you understand these origins, you can question them and potentially loosen their grip.

---

3. The Harmful Effects of Persistent Shame

Shame does more than just make you feel bad. It can lead to a cycle of withdrawal, preventing you from trying new things or reaching out for help. You might feel you do not deserve success, so you do not pursue better opportunities. In relationships, shame can cause you to hide your feelings, push people away, or accept poor treatment because you think you have no value.

Shame can also fuel harmful coping mechanisms—substance misuse, disordered eating, or other behaviors aimed at numbing emotional pain. These coping methods can create new regrets, reinforcing the shame in a repeating loop. Over time, persistent shame leads to isolation, low self-esteem, and a sense that life is limited by your perceived flaws. Breaking free requires identifying shame's role in your actions and mental habits.

---

4. Shifting from Shame to Responsibility

A useful step is to transform shame into responsibility. Instead of saying, "I am worthless," you say, "I did something harmful, and I can do better." This subtle change moves the focus from your entire being to specific actions. You no longer define yourself by the mistake; rather, you look at what you can correct or avoid next time.

- **Name the Action, Not the Self**: If you regret a betrayal, recognize it as a betrayal, not as proof that you are an irredeemable traitor. Then consider the steps to fix or avoid repeating it.
- **Avoid Labels**: Words like "failure," "monster," or "lazy" turn the entire identity negative. Replace them with statements about a single behavior: "I failed that test," or "I did not prepare well for that task." This approach keeps you from exaggerating the mistake into a permanent label.
- **Plan for Improvement**: Even small steps—like reading a related book or talking to a mentor—signal that you can act differently. Shame weakens when you see concrete evidence of growth.

By focusing on responsibility for actions, you create hope. Mistakes are no longer final verdicts on your character; they are problems you can address.

5. Building Self-Compassion to Counter Shame

Self-compassion is a powerful antidote to shame because it combines kindness toward yourself with acceptance that you are human and prone to error. While guilt might remain as a useful signal to avoid certain behavior, shame recedes when you treat yourself as someone worthy of a second chance.

- **Supportive Inner Voice**: Speak to yourself as you would to a close friend who is hurting. Instead of, "I can't believe how foolish I am," say, "I made an error, but I can learn from it like anyone else."
- **Physical Reminders**: Sometimes placing a hand on your chest or giving yourself a gentle hug can create a calming effect, reinforcing the idea that you deserve warmth and understanding. This physical gesture might feel awkward, but many find it grounding.
- **Common Humanity**: Remember that everyone has regrets, flaws, and embarrassing experiences. Shame tries to convince you that you are uniquely broken, but in reality, imperfection is universal.

Self-compassion is not self-indulgence. It is a balanced view that acknowledges mistakes while still granting yourself basic respect. Over time, this approach to your inner voice can gradually melt the layers of shame.

---

6. Challenging the Inner Critic

An intense inner critic amplifies shame by repeating negative judgments. It might say, "You will never succeed," or "Everyone can see how terrible you are." Recognizing that this voice is not the absolute truth is a key step toward releasing shame.

- **Name Your Critic**: Give it a label like "the harsh judge." Each time you catch that voice making a blanket statement, you can respond, "That is the harsh judge again. I do not have to believe it."
- **Collect Counter-Evidence**: For each negative statement ("I always fail"), look for times you did well, even if they seem minor. Writing down counter-examples can break the critic's illusion of total correctness.
- **Stay in Facts**: The inner critic often uses exaggerated phrases like "always" or "never." Replace them with measured observations: "I failed this time, but that does not mean I always will."

By consciously replying to the inner critic, you train your mind to challenge shame rather than accept it passively.

---

7. Seeking Safe Outlets to Talk About Shame

Shame thrives in secrecy. Talking openly, even to one supportive person, can bring relief. The listener's nonjudgmental response can confirm that your perceived defect is not as final or terrible as you feared.

- **Close Friends or Family**: Pick someone you trust not to minimize or mock your feelings. Explain that you want to share a vulnerable topic. Their empathy might crack the shell of shame.
- **Support Groups**: If your shame is related to a specific issue—like addiction or a history of a mistake—groups exist where people

understand your struggle. Listening to their stories can also show you that you are not alone.
- **Professional Counselors**: Trained therapists provide a structured space to explore shame without condemnation. They can help you identify the sources and practice new ways of thinking about your self-worth.

Hiding shame can deepen it. Bringing it to the light of a compassionate conversation is a major step toward healing.

---

8. Body-Based Approaches to Easing Shame

Shame is not just a mental state; it can also appear as physical tension, aches, or a sense of heaviness. Certain body-based methods can reduce these physical symptoms and, in turn, lower the intensity of shame in the mind.

- **Grounding Techniques**: Stand or sit with your feet firmly on the floor. Pay attention to the contact points—your feet on the ground, your back against a chair. Slowly breathe, telling yourself you are safe in the present moment.
- **Gentle Movement**: Activities like yoga, stretching, or slow walks can release stored tension. Focusing on the body's sensations can break the loop of shame-based thoughts.
- **Relaxation Exercises**: Tensing and releasing muscle groups from head to toe relaxes the body, sending calming signals to the brain. This can create a less receptive environment for shame messages.

By caring for your physical state, you reduce the power shame has to dominate your emotional state.

---

9. Turning Shame into Empathy for Others

When you have experienced deep shame, you might become more understanding of others facing similar feelings. This empathy can help counter your own shame by shifting some of your focus outward.

- **Volunteer Work**: Helping others who struggle—whether it is tutoring, emotional support, or community service—can give you a sense of

purpose. You realize you can contribute good to the world, countering shame's message that you are worthless.
- **Supportive Listening**: When friends or acquaintances share regrets, you can offer a truly sympathetic ear. Your personal experience with shame means you can relate and reassure them that mistakes do not define a person forever.
- **Shared Healing**: In some cases, forming a small circle—either in person or online—where everyone talks about shame can be transformative. By voicing your stories, you help each other let go of the intense isolation shame creates.

Using shame as a bridge to empathy does not erase your own pain, but it lessens the sense that you are uniquely flawed. You see that everyone carries emotional burdens, and together, those burdens can be eased.

---

10. Rewriting Your Inner Story

Shame often roots itself in the story we tell about ourselves. Maybe you keep replaying a single worst moment as proof you are "bad." Changing this narrative does not mean denying the mistake; it means placing it in a fuller context.

- **A Wider Perspective**: Write a short personal history that includes your strengths, successes, helpful acts, and times of resilience. Include the regretful moments too, but see them as parts of a whole life story, not the sole highlight.
- **Update Self-Labels**: Instead of "I am forever a cheater," try "I cheated once in a past relationship, which taught me how vital honesty is to me now." This shift acknowledges the action without locking you into that identity forever.
- **Seek Encouraging Examples**: Look up stories of well-known people who made big errors yet turned their lives around. Their arcs might inspire you to reshape your own narrative from one of shame to one of learning.

Each time you notice your internal story returning to a shameful loop, remind yourself that you have the right to edit and expand your personal storyline.

---

11. Dealing with Public or Community-Based Shame

At times, shame is magnified by public knowledge of your mistake—maybe it was local gossip, an online scandal, or legal trouble. You may feel branded by your past in your community. While this is certainly harder to face, it is still possible to reduce the weight of shame.

- **Own Your Story Publicly**: If appropriate, you might state your side of the story in a measured way—acknowledging the mistake but highlighting the steps you have taken to make amends. This transparency can prevent rumors from defining you.
- **Selective Engagement**: In some situations, you may choose to withdraw from certain social circles or online forums if they keep shaming you. You have a right to protect your mental health, even if others do not offer understanding.
- **Find Fresh Environments**: Sometimes a new job, a different neighborhood, or an online community of supportive individuals can give you space to rebuild your self-image without constant reminders of the old situation.
- **Mental Rehearsal**: If you must stay in the same place, practice how you will respond to curious or judgmental questions. A brief, calm answer like, "Yes, I made a serious mistake, and I have taken steps to change," can help you feel more prepared.

By navigating public shame with self-control and honesty, you lessen its power to define you. Over time, many communities move on, and you can integrate the lessons of your past without letting it overshadow everything else.

---

12. Re-Evaluating Your Personal Values

Sometimes shame indicates a disconnect between your actions and your personal values. If you continue feeling shame after apologizing and making amends, it might be time to re-examine what you truly stand for.

- **List Your Core Values**: Honesty, responsibility, kindness, perseverance, family, etc. Reflect on how your regretful action contrasted with these values.

- **Align with Positive Actions**: Create small goals that show you are living according to these values now. For instance, if you value generosity, find ways to share resources or volunteer.
- **Accept Personal Growth**: Realize that values can be shaped by regrets. If you once cheated in a contest and now you deeply value fairness, see that shift as evidence of positive character evolution. Shame can weaken when you see that your core principles are stronger than before.

Living in line with your values going forward allows you to stop viewing your old mistake as your eternal identity. You can see it as a turning point toward authenticity and a more aligned life.

---

13. Setting Healthy Boundaries with People Who Shame You

In some cases, certain individuals repeatedly remind you of your past mistake, using it as a weapon. They might hold it over your head or belittle you. This behavior can trap you in a shame cycle, making it difficult to move on. Addressing it might require assertiveness:

- **Speak Up**: Calmly tell them that their repeated reminders are not helping you grow. If they continue, you may need to reduce contact or set clear rules about which topics are off-limits.
- **Reality Check**: Sometimes people shame you to control you. Recognize that this says more about them than it does about your worth.
- **Self-Protective Measures**: If they will not stop, consider limiting how often you interact or even cutting ties if the relationship is purely damaging. Your emotional health must take priority over someone else's desire to judge.

Building a new relationship with yourself sometimes requires distancing from those who prefer you remain stuck in shame.

---

14. Small Steps to Restore Self-Worth

Recovering from lingering shame takes time. Setting small, achievable tasks can gradually repair your self-image. Each completed step contradicts the shame narrative that says you "cannot do anything right."

- **Daily Acts of Kindness**: This might be as simple as complimenting a colleague or helping a neighbor carry groceries. Observing yourself doing kind acts counters the belief that you are a terrible person.
- **Learning a New Skill**: Shame often says, "You are incapable." Acquiring even a basic skill—like cooking a new dish or fixing a household item—proves you can improve. This sense of competence chips away at shame.
- **Writing Affirmations**: Each evening, list three things you handled decently that day. They do not have to be big. Over time, this consistent practice builds evidence of your reliability and worth.

Focusing on small wins helps shift attention from your perceived flaws to genuine capabilities. It is not about ignoring your mistakes but about recognizing that shame's negative verdict is not the whole truth.

---

15. Using Regret as a Guide, Not a Prison

Shame can lock you into a prison of inaction. You might avoid any new situations for fear of messing up again. Yet, regret can be turned into a guide that shows you what matters to you. If you feel shame about lying, it might reveal that integrity is important to you. Instead of dwelling on your past failure, use that insight to make honesty a non-negotiable part of your future.

- **Focus on the Lesson**: "What did this regret teach me about my true priorities?" Shift your energy from punishing yourself to applying the lesson in daily life.
- **Give Yourself Permission to Try**: If you fear failure, remind yourself that mistakes are part of learning. Shame tries to freeze you in place, but living by your deeper values means taking risks again.
- **Release External Approval**: Sometimes shame is connected to letting others down. While you can respect their opinions, your healing depends on your own judgment of your path. If you fixate on their view of you, you stay locked in the past.

By turning regret into a guide, you replace self-condemnation with purposeful action. Each time you live by the lesson you learned, you undermine shame's hold.

16. Therapy Approaches for Deep-Seated Shame

For longstanding shame—especially from childhood trauma, repeated bullying, or a history of serious mistakes—self-help steps might not be enough. Therapy can delve into deeper layers.

- **Cognitive Behavioral Therapy (CBT)**: Helps identify distorted thoughts causing shame and replaces them with balanced perspectives. You challenge the "I am worthless" narrative through evidence-based exercises.
- **Eye Movement Desensitization and Reprocessing (EMDR)**: Used often for trauma. It can help reframe painful memories so that they lose their intensity. While the memory remains, the crippling shame can reduce over time.
- **Schema Therapy**: Focuses on core beliefs formed in early life. A therapist guides you to see how those beliefs lead to shame and helps you restructure them.
- **Mindfulness-Based Approaches**: Learning to observe your thoughts without judgment can break the cycle of self-blame. Over time, you respond more gently to feelings of shame, letting them pass rather than consume you.

A qualified mental health professional can tailor methods to your specific background, ensuring you address both the emotional scars and the thinking patterns that maintain shame.

17. Preventing Relapse into Shame

Even after making significant progress, certain triggers—an old friend, a place with bad memories—can resurrect shame. Having a plan to handle these triggers is important.

- **Stay Mindful of Warning Signs**: Notice if your thoughts begin spiraling with negative self-talk. Early detection allows you to respond with the coping methods you have learned, such as positive self-statements or a quick call to a supportive friend.

- **Adjust to New Life Stages**: Shame might reappear when you move into a different phase, like a new job or parenthood, because it revives old doubts. Revisit your therapy notes or self-help strategies to reinforce your healthier mindset.
- **Ongoing Self-Reflection**: A short weekly check can help you catch creeping shame. Ask, "Have I been unusually harsh with myself this week?" If so, apply your known tools—journaling, affirmations, or a talk with a mentor—before it escalates.

Remaining aware of potential backslides keeps you from feeling like a failure if shame resurfaces. It is normal for old patterns to flare up under stress. With a proactive plan, you can avoid sinking back into the same depth.

---

18. Conclusion of Chapter 16

Lingering shame can be one of the most stubborn aspects of regret, often outlasting the actual mistake or any external consequences. It latches onto your identity and whispers that you are unworthy or inherently flawed. However, by differentiating shame from guilt, identifying its sources, and actively confronting the distorted beliefs that feed it, you can begin to shake free of its hold. Tools like self-compassion, open communication, therapy, and daily affirming actions serve as pathways out of shame's shadows.

Progress takes time, particularly if shame has been part of your life for years or even decades. But each moment you question a harsh self-judgment or act in line with your core values, you weaken shame's influence. Gradually, you can see yourself as a fallible yet still fundamentally valuable person. Instead of viewing your mistakes as proof of your failings, they become signals for growth and empathy—for yourself and for others going through similar battles. In this way, shame no longer rules your life, and you reclaim the freedom to move forward without the crushing burden of self-condemnation.

CHAPTER 17: STRENGTHENING PROBLEM-SOLVING SKILLS

Regret often appears when we feel stuck in a situation or have trouble dealing with unexpected events. Learning to solve problems effectively can prevent regrets from forming in the first place, and it can also help address any issues that arise from regrets we already carry. By developing strong methods to identify, analyze, and tackle challenges, we gain a sense of control that counters the helplessness sometimes tied to regret. This chapter provides detailed strategies to improve problem-solving skills, shows why they matter for long-term peace of mind, and shares ways to apply them to everyday dilemmas.

1. Understanding the Connection Between Regret and Problem-Solving

Many regrets come from moments when we were not equipped to handle an obstacle or crisis. Perhaps we rushed into a decision without weighing important details, or we froze when forced to act quickly. Strengthening your ability to solve problems lowers the odds of making rash moves. It also replaces panic or avoidance with structured thinking. In everyday life, effective problem-solving helps you assess potential risks, find meaningful options, and reduce the chance of lingering remorse.

Moreover, regrets can often be undone or softened by a fresh problem-solving effort. If you regret handling a conflict poorly, applying methodical reasoning can guide you in making amends or preventing the same mistake in future. Rather than dwelling on what went wrong, you can break the issue into smaller parts, tackle each piece, and take small steps to fix or at least limit the damage. This proactive mindset is key to escaping the passive feeling of being trapped by regretful memories.

2. Identifying the Real Problem

Sometimes the first hurdle is figuring out the root problem rather than a symptom. You might see that you have lingering arguments with a coworker, but the true problem could be role confusion in the team or unspoken resentment from a past incident. Addressing symptoms only leads to temporary relief. For instance, if you regret frequent clashes with a friend, you could keep apologizing each time. But unless you discover the underlying reason—maybe your schedules keep conflicting, leading to stress that sparks arguments—the pattern might continue.

To find the real problem:

- **Ask "Why" Repeatedly**: If you notice you are always behind on a project, ask why you are behind. If the answer is, "I procrastinate," ask why you procrastinate. Keep going until you land on a fundamental cause, such as fear of failing or unclear objectives.
- **Look for Patterns**: If the same regret or conflict keeps popping up with different people or in different settings, you might share a trait or habit that causes it. Spotting these patterns helps you identify the deeper source.
- **Gather Input from Others**: Sometimes friends, family, or coworkers can see the root problem more clearly than we do. Their observations can shed light on an angle you missed.

Understanding the real issue prevents you from wasting time on side matters and ensures that your efforts go into genuine resolution. This skill is vital for addressing regrets because many regrets linger when the underlying cause remains hidden or ignored.

---

3. Breaking Down Large Problems into Manageable Parts

A major reason we fail to solve problems is feeling overwhelmed by their size. Large tasks can block our ability to think calmly, leading to rushed or avoidant behavior that often results in regret. The solution is to decompose big problems into smaller, more approachable tasks:

- **List All Components**: Write down every step or piece of the situation that concerns you. For example, if the problem involves a complex home renovation you regret starting, list all sub-tasks (budgeting, contractor selection, timeline management, alternative plans, and so on).

- **Prioritize**: Decide which parts need immediate attention and which can wait. Handling urgent aspects first prevents them from causing further chaos, while giving you room to plan out the less critical pieces.
- **Set Micro-Deadlines**: Instead of telling yourself, "I will fix the entire problem by next month," pick smaller deadlines for each sub-task. This keeps you motivated and reduces the sense of chaos.

Breaking a big problem into smaller units allows you to act methodically. Each small success reduces stress and counters the sense of helplessness that triggers regretful decisions. Over time, this habit trains your mind to tackle challenges with composure.

---

4. Structured Methods for Problem-Solving

Several classic approaches exist to guide you through systematic problem-solving. Applying these methods can be especially helpful when regret stems from impulsive or poorly informed choices. By adopting a proven framework, you train yourself to slow down and weigh possibilities more carefully.

4.1 The IDEAL Model

- **I**dentify the problem
- **D**efine goals and outcomes
- **E**xplore possible strategies
- **A**ct on the chosen strategy
- **L**ook back to evaluate results

This model reminds you to clarify both the issue and your desired end state before jumping to solutions. If you find that your chosen fix is not working, step back to the "Explore" stage and consider an alternative.

4.2 The "Five Whys" Approach

As mentioned, keep asking "why" until you uncover a root cause. This keeps you from slapping a bandage on symptoms. For instance, if you regret not finishing a project on time, ask why. If the answer is "I got distracted," ask why you got distracted. Continue until you find that maybe your workspace is too noisy or your project goals are unclear. Once you find the fundamental issue, you can address it directly.

4.3 SWOT Analysis

While often used in business, a quick SWOT (Strengths, Weaknesses, Opportunities, Threats) analysis can clarify options:

- **Strengths**: What advantages do you have in solving this problem?
- **Weaknesses**: Which internal factors might slow or block you?
- **Opportunities**: Are there external resources or supportive conditions you can use?
- **Threats**: Which external risks or negative forces could harm your efforts?

Seeing these categories laid out helps you pick a path that leverages your strengths and reduces risks, lowering the chance of new regrets.

---

5. Gathering and Evaluating Information

One cause of regret is making decisions on limited or incorrect data. If you want to solve a problem correctly, you must gather enough facts or seek reliable opinions first. This can range from simple research (such as reading consumer reviews before a purchase) to more complex investigations (like consulting subject experts).

- **Varied Sources**: Avoid relying on a single individual or website. Cross-check details to see if they line up. If the stakes are high—such as a legal or medical issue—consult more than one professional.
- **Deep Listening**: When people involved in the problem share their views, do not just hear; really listen. Their perspective might highlight angles you never considered.
- **Identifying Gaps**: Note any missing information. For example, if you plan to switch careers but have not looked at the job market or salary ranges, that gap can lead to regret later if your new path is not viable.
- **Logical vs. Emotional Data**: Emotional insights (like how a choice aligns with your values) are valid, but they should sit alongside practical data. Combining both lowers the risk of regretful outcomes.

If you sense a creeping feeling that you do not know enough, treat that as a sign to pause and research further. A short delay for more information might save you from a long period of regret.

6. Collaborative Problem-Solving

Sometimes you face problems that affect others—like family disputes, group projects, or community issues. Solving these alone can be tough, and misunderstandings might spark further regrets. Collaborative problem-solving engages all parties in finding a shared resolution:

- **Group Discussion**: Hold a calm meeting or conversation where everyone can share their concerns and ideas without interruption. This fosters collective understanding.
- **Brainstorm Together**: Encourage everyone to propose solutions, even those that seem unusual. The combined creativity can reveal options no single person would have seen alone.
- **Assign Clear Roles**: Once you pick a plan, ensure each participant knows their tasks and deadlines. Vagueness can cause future conflicts, leading to regrets.
- **Agree on Follow-Up**: Set a time to check progress as a group. This step keeps the plan on track and prevents small snags from becoming big obstacles.

Working as a team can reduce blame and the regret that stems from feeling alone in fixing a crisis. However, it requires good communication and a willingness to share credit for successes or own up to missteps if they occur.

7. Overcoming Emotional Blocks to Problem-Solving

Even if you know the right steps, emotions like fear, embarrassment, or anger can disrupt logical thinking. An angry mind may rush into harmful solutions. A scared mind might avoid the issue, causing regrets from inaction. Recognizing these emotional blocks is crucial:

- **Pause and Cool Down**: If you are upset, take a short break. Engage in a calming exercise—deep breathing, a short walk, or even a few quiet moments. With a clearer head, you can resume problem-solving.
- **Name Your Feeling**: Simply stating "I feel anxious about making a mistake" helps you see it as an emotion, not a fact. Once identified, you can address the fear instead of letting it control you.
- **Reality Testing**: Ask yourself how likely the worst outcome really is. Often, we magnify small risks under stress. Gaining perspective reduces panic-based choices that lead to regret.
- **Seek Support**: If your emotions are too strong, talk to a friend, counselor, or advisor who can offer a calmer viewpoint.

Practicing emotional regulation during problem-solving does not mean ignoring feelings; it means acknowledging them without letting them hijack the process. This balance can save you from decisions you would regret later.

---

8. Thinking Ahead: Considering Future Consequences

A big cause of regret is failing to anticipate long-term outcomes. People might jump at an immediate reward or relief, only to discover lasting drawbacks. Adding a future-thinking step to your problem-solving can help:

- **Short-Term vs. Long-Term Analysis**: Weigh the immediate benefits of a solution against its future downsides. For example, an impulsive purchase might offer quick satisfaction but harm your budget in the long run.
- **Ripple Effect**: Ask how your choice might affect other areas of life—work, family, health. A local fix could create broader issues later. If you are deciding to relocate for a job, consider how it impacts your family's routines and your social ties.
- **Best-Case, Worst-Case, Middle Scenario**: Picture each scenario in a few months or a year. This mental exercise can reduce regrets by revealing paths that are obviously too risky or unsustainable.
- **Adaptability**: Sometimes you cannot predict everything. Build in a fallback plan or exit strategy. If the first path fails, you can shift without catastrophe.

By extending your view beyond the next few weeks, you avoid the myopic approach that fuels many regrets. You also allow yourself to spot hidden costs or unexpected rewards in each option.

9. Practicing Decision-Making Under Pressure

High-pressure situations—like final exam days, urgent deadlines, or sudden crises—often lead to hasty decisions that spawn regret. You can prepare for these scenarios through practice and simulation:

- **Timed Drills**: If you know your job or lifestyle involves quick decisions, you can rehearse. Set a timer, state a mock problem, then challenge yourself to propose a solution in a few minutes. Over time, your mind learns to stay cool under a ticking clock.
- **Partial Information Exercises**: In real life, you rarely have every detail. Practice making the best choice with incomplete facts. This skill prevents panic when you do not have perfect data.
- **Post-Action Reviews**: After each drill (or real urgent decision), review what went well and what could improve. This reflection cements good habits and reduces the odds of repeating poor ones.

Nerves and stress do not automatically doom you to regrets. With training, you can maintain a structured approach even when the clock is running fast.

10. Learning from Mistakes and Adjusting

Even top-tier problem-solving does not guarantee perfect outcomes. Sometimes the chosen solution fails or introduces new complications. The difference between repeated regrets and learning lies in how you handle these results:

- **Feedback Loops**: As soon as you see how your solution performs, note the positives and negatives. Did it fix the main issue? Did it create side effects you had not anticipated?
- **Stay Flexible**: If results are poor, do not double down out of pride. Return to your problem-solving method, consider new data, and pick a different path. Stubbornly clinging to a failing plan often leads to deeper regrets.

- **Recognize Small Wins**: Recognize incremental successes or partial fixes. Even if the entire plan did not succeed, identifying what did work helps your morale and guides you on what to keep next time.
- **Document Lessons**: For complex problems, keep a short record of what happened, which approach you tried, and how it ended. This "problem-solving journal" becomes a resource for future challenges.

Approaching failures as data for refinement, rather than proof of your incompetence, can drastically reduce the emotional sting of regret. It reframes mistakes as stepping stones toward better skills.

---

11. Building Mental Agility Through Puzzles and Exercises

Problem-solving is like a muscle: practice strengthens it. Outside of real-world challenges, you can stretch your mind with exercises and mental games that boost your creative thinking, logical reasoning, and flexibility.

- **Brain Teasers**: Classic puzzles—logic riddles, lateral thinking tasks, or numeric sequences—train you to see patterns and question assumptions. This habit carries over into daily life.
- **Strategy Games**: Activities like chess, sudoku, or certain board games teach long-term planning and risk management. You learn to consider multiple angles and stay aware of changing conditions.
- **Creative Challenges**: Engaging in small design or innovation tasks—like building something from scratch or writing a short problem-solving story—pushes your mind to generate ideas spontaneously.

While these may seem like leisure activities, they can sharpen problem-solving instincts in a low-stress environment. Over time, these instincts help you handle real dilemmas with more confidence and fewer regrets.

---

12. Strengthening Communication Skills for Shared Problems

Even if you solve issues well individually, real-life situations often require input or buy-in from others. If you are not skilled at communication, your solution might flop due to poor presentation or misunderstandings.

- **Clarity and Brevity**: Explain your ideas in straightforward language. Rambling speeches confuse people, leading to half-hearted support.
- **Focus on Benefits**: When suggesting a fix, highlight how it helps everyone, not just you. This inclusive angle builds cooperation rather than suspicion.
- **Active Listening (Again)**: If colleagues or family members give counterpoints, truly listen. Incorporate valid points into your plan. This inclusive approach often refines the final solution and reduces the chance of future regrets.
- **Conflict Resolution Tools**: Know how to mediate differences or defuse tension. For instance, repeating the other person's view in your own words before offering your perspective can lower defensiveness.

If you have a habit of imposing decisions, regrets can emerge later when resentful parties sabotage or refuse to follow the plan. Good communication ensures that everyone feels involved and thus more likely to support the final outcome.

---

13. Avoiding Over-Analysis and Indecision

While thorough thinking is crucial, some people get trapped in over-analysis—endlessly weighing pros and cons until deadlines pass. This "analysis paralysis" can also lead to regret, as you miss chances due to fear of picking the wrong path.

- **Set Reasonable Limits**: Decide on a period for research or reflection. Once that period ends, act on your best insight. In many cases, 80% of the needed information is enough to make a sound choice.
- **Trust Experience**: If you have knowledge or past practice in a certain area, let that guide you. Endless data collection might not change the final decision significantly.
- **Satisficing**: This idea means picking an option that satisfies the main criteria even if it is not perfect. Constantly searching for the ultimate perfect choice is often unrealistic and can breed regret when you never actually commit.
- **Self-Check for Anxiety**: If you hesitate too long, ask if fear of failure is fueling your delay. Recognizing this can push you to decide and accept that no path is risk-free.

Striking a balance between diligence and timely action prevents regrets on both sides—rushing in blindly versus missing the moment altogether.

---

14. Handling Uncontrollable Factors

Sometimes, regrets stem from external factors—an economic downturn, a sudden accident, or a policy change beyond your control. Good problem-solving acknowledges what you cannot alter and focuses on what you can.

- **Acceptance**: Recognize that no approach guarantees success if huge outside forces are at play. This acceptance lowers self-blame for outcomes you truly could not affect.
- **Contingency Planning**: If you sense external risk, plan for worst-case scenarios. This readiness reduces shock if the risk becomes real, and you can shift to a fallback option quickly.
- **Adaptive Mindset**: If events turn against you, do not cling to old methods. Pause, reassess, and realign your solution to the new environment. Sticking with a path that no longer fits reality only produces more regret.
- **Emotional Resilience**: Develop the mental habit of understanding that outside events do not always reflect your personal worth or skill. Keep regrets in perspective by noting that you did your part responsibly.

By distinguishing between what you can and cannot change, you keep regret from spiraling into personal failure narratives.

---

15. Teaching Problem-Solving to Others

One powerful way to reinforce your own skills is teaching them. When you guide a friend, child, or coworker through systematic problem-solving, you cement the steps in your own mind. This reciprocal benefit also fosters an environment where everyone is better at handling issues—lowering collective regrets in a household or team.

- **Model the Process**: If someone asks for help, walk them through your method step by step. Let them see how you define the problem, gather info, brainstorm, and choose an option.

- **Ask Leading Questions**: Instead of giving answers outright, pose questions that direct them to discover solutions. This approach builds their confidence and understanding.
- **Recognize Their Efforts**: Recognize small improvements they make, which motivates them to keep practicing. Let them know problem-solving is a learned skill, not a talent granted at birth.

Teaching others not only improves their outcomes but also keeps you consistent. If you slip into poor patterns yourself, you will recognize the mismatch between what you teach and what you do, prompting you to stay true to best practices.

---

16. Building a Reputation for Fair Solutions

As you polish your problem-solving skills, you might find others increasingly seek your input. Being seen as someone who handles conflicts or challenges calmly and fairly can open doors in personal and professional spheres. People trust a mind that systematically weighs options instead of reacting emotionally. This trust can protect you from regrets related to damaged reputations or lost opportunities.

- **Stay Ethical**: Resist shortcuts or manipulative tactics. If you craft solutions that benefit you at the expense of others, you may face regrets later when distrust forms.
- **Involve Stakeholders**: When a problem affects multiple people, reflect their views in the solution. This inclusive approach builds a positive image and fosters lasting goodwill.
- **Maintain Transparency**: If you are uncertain about some aspects, admit it. Pretending you know everything can lead to bigger regrets if your plan fails. Showing honesty about limits earns respect and extra support.
- **Keep Learning**: Even experts refine their methods. Continual learning—reading about conflict management, attending seminars—ensures you do not become complacent. The more robust your skills, the fewer regrets you will have about missed angles or unplanned risks.

A solid reputation for fair problem-solving is a shield against many regrets. It surrounds you with cooperative allies instead of resentful adversaries.

17. Integrating Problem-Solving into Daily Routines

Making problem-solving part of your everyday life cements it as a core skill rather than an occasional tactic. This integration prevents regrets caused by hasty actions in routine matters, such as budgeting, scheduling, or even personal health choices.

- **Morning or Weekly Review**: Set aside a small block of time to review upcoming tasks or potential challenges. Spotting them early lets you plan and reduce surprises.
- **Checklist for Frequent Issues**: If you repeatedly face the same type of problem—like forgetting to pay bills on time—create a quick reference list. Include steps to gather necessary info, evaluate payment options, and finalize payment. Each time you follow the list, you sharpen the habit.
- **Share with Household Members**: If you live with family or roommates, encourage them to use structured problem-solving too. Aligning methods at home can cut down on petty conflicts and regrets over disorganized living.
- **Debrief Evening**: Spend a few minutes at the end of the day checking if any small problems arose. Did you handle them well, or could you apply a better approach next time? This reflection helps you catch and correct patterns before regret grows.

Routinely practicing these steps ensures that logic and clarity guide you, even in small daily choices. Over time, this pattern fosters confidence in your decision-making process and reduces the likelihood of regrets stacking up.

18. Conclusion of Chapter 17

Strengthening problem-solving skills offers a powerful defense against the sense of helplessness that often fuels regret. By learning to dissect challenges, gather the right information, and methodically pick and test solutions, you transform potential pitfalls into manageable tasks. Good problem-solving also helps you repair past regrets by giving you a structured way to address lingering issues, whether they are conflicts with others or personal dilemmas.

The strategies described here—from breaking large problems into small chunks to practicing under timed conditions—enhance your mental discipline and emotional balance. They make you more likely to act with foresight instead of impulse and to adjust smoothly when circumstances shift. Over the long run, these habits foster self-trust and reduce the heavy mental load of repeated regrets. While you cannot erase all mistakes from your life, systematic problem-solving ensures that each lesson guides you toward wiser decisions, leading to a calmer and more fulfilling path.

CHAPTER 18: MAINTAINING HOPE IN DAILY LIFE

For those struggling with regret, one of the hardest tasks is keeping a sense of hope. Regret can darken your perspective, making it seem like past mistakes limit all future chances. Yet a hopeful outlook is not naive. It is a practical tool that helps you see possibilities, stay motivated, and find meaning despite setbacks. This chapter explains how to build and maintain hope as part of your regular routine, how to handle cynicism and negative self-talk, and why hopefulness is an essential ally in overcoming regrets.

1. Defining Hope as an Active Mindset

Hope is not just wishing for good outcomes; it is the belief, backed by intention, that you can pursue meaningful goals and adapt when faced with challenges. This definition distinguishes hope from mere optimism or "positive thinking." Hope involves an active component: planning how to move forward, even in uncertain times. In contrast, mere positive thinking might ignore real issues or rely on luck. By actively nurturing hope, you reduce the tendency to see regrets as final verdicts on your future.

2. Why Hope Matters for Regret Recovery

Regret is draining because it focuses on lost opportunities or mistakes you cannot fully undo. This backward-looking lens can block your view of future possibilities, causing a sense of doom. Hope reorients your sight toward what you can still achieve or experience. It does not deny that you made errors; rather, it acknowledges them while claiming there is still room for progress.

- **Motivation to Act**: Hope spurs effort. Without hope, you might give up on solutions or dwell on blame. If you believe a better outcome is possible, you are more inclined to put in the necessary work—like seeking therapy, trying new strategies, or apologizing to mend relationships.
- **Emotional Resilience**: Hope buffers you against despair. Even if a plan fails, hope says you can adapt and try again. This resilience prevents a single setback from turning into a permanent regretful mindset.

- **Health Benefits**: Studies suggest that hopeful people often cope better with stress and show stronger immune responses. While not a magic cure, hope supports overall well-being, making it easier to face challenges.
- **Improved Relationships**: Hopeful individuals tend to communicate with more optimism, attracting supportive allies rather than pushing others away with cynicism.

By fostering hope, you nurture a mental environment where regret does not overshadow everything else. You give regrets a place as lessons, not as the end of the story.

---

3. Understanding Realistic Hope vs. Blind Optimism

One reason some people reject hope is that they confuse it with denial of reality. They worry that being hopeful means ignoring real problems or sugarcoating serious issues. Actually, realistic hope acknowledges difficulties while still believing that positive outcomes can emerge with effort and adaptation.

- **Accepting Facts**: For instance, if you regret not pursuing a particular career, realistic hope means you accept it might be harder now, but you still consider possible steps—further education, new networking, or a related path—rather than assuming it is forever impossible.
- **Flexible Goals**: Realistic hope is open to adjusting targets. If one door closes, it looks for another opening instead of clinging to a single dream that might be outdated. This adaptability avoids the bitterness that can come from hoping for the impossible.
- **Self-Honesty**: Blind optimism might pretend your regrets never happened or that they have zero impact. Realistic hope says, "Yes, this event shaped me, but I can still move on with new insights." That mix of truth and forward momentum keeps hope stable.
- **Balanced Risk-Taking**: You still measure potential downsides. Hope does not require jumping blindly into huge gambles. Instead, it weighs options with a sense that some path forward is likely to exist.

By practicing realistic hope, you avoid falling into either extreme—cynical defeat or naive fantasies. You find a middle ground that helps you handle regret effectively.

4. Daily Habits That Support a Hopeful Outlook

Cultivating hope does not rely on a single grand gesture. It grows through small, regular habits that shape how you view yourself and your prospects. Here are ways to keep hope alive each day:

- **Morning Intention**: Start by identifying one positive aim for the day, even if minor—like reaching out to a friend or making progress on a personal project. This sets a constructive tone.
- **Exposure to Uplifting Material**: Seek books, articles, or podcasts that discuss real stories of people overcoming adversity. Their experiences can remind you that transformation is possible.
- **Mindful Breathing**: In times of hopelessness, the mind often churns with negative images. Taking a few minutes to breathe slowly and focus on the present can calm those images, making space for more hopeful thoughts.
- **Small Acts of Kindness**: Doing something helpful for someone else—even if it is just sending an encouraging note—reinforces the idea that positive impact is within your control. This sense of agency supports hope.
- **Regular Recognitions**: Recognize small wins. If you consistently do not see your achievements, you might feel life is static. By noticing each tiny success, you strengthen the conviction that progress is ongoing.

When these habits become second nature, your mind is less prone to spiral into despair over regrets. You have ongoing evidence that positive change happens in your everyday life.

5. Handling Negativity and Cynicism

Hope can feel fragile in an environment or mental climate of negativity. Perhaps your social circle is prone to pessimistic chatter, or you have an internal voice that mocks hopeful aspirations. Learning to navigate these influences is crucial:

- **Limit Exposure**: If certain acquaintances only complain and never consider solutions, reduce how often you engage in those conversations. This does not mean you abandon friends, but you can steer topics or gently set boundaries.

- **Challenge Cynical Thoughts**: When a cynical notion arises—"It will never work"—test it. Is that based on fact, or fear? Recall examples where attempts did yield results, even if partial. This mental shift prevents cynical statements from becoming your default.
- **Counterbalance with Action**: Sometimes cynicism is fed by stagnation. Show yourself evidence of movement. Even a small step toward improvement, like updating your résumé or practicing a new skill, counters the narrative that "nothing changes."
- **Seek Hopeful Allies**: Spend time with people who share a can-do attitude without ignoring real problems. Their perspective can remind you that hope is not foolish. They may also provide practical tips that confirm optimism can lead to tangible benefits.

Gradually, you can reshape the mental and social environment so that cynicism holds less power. This shift makes it easier to stay hopeful when regrets threaten to overshadow your forward momentum.

---

6. Reframing Regret as a Pathway to Growth

Hope is more robust when you see regrets not as dead ends, but as catalysts for growth. This reframing approach acknowledges the past mistake but focuses on the improved insight or skill you can gain from it. For example, if you regret ignoring health warnings, you can frame it as the event that sparked long-term healthy habits.

- **Identify the Lesson**: Name one concrete lesson each significant regret taught you. Maybe you learned the importance of planning or the value of honest communication. Write this lesson down so you do not forget it.
- **Apply It Purposefully**: Each time you face a new choice that vaguely resembles the old scenario, remind yourself of the lesson. For instance, if your regret was about rushing into decisions, you can actively slow your decision process in the future.
- **Teach Others**: Sharing your regret story and the resulting lesson can solidify it in your mind while helping others avoid similar mistakes. This outward sharing transforms regret into a beneficial resource for your social circle.
- **Track Transformations**: Keep note of any positive changes you made that directly stem from regret. Over time, you may see that what once felt like

a final failure has become a stepping stone to better living, reinforcing hope in your ability to adapt.

This perspective does not trivialize the pain of regret. It simply ensures that your mistakes fuel constructive changes rather than lifelong self-blame.

---

7. Embracing Small Indicators of Progress

One reason people lose hope is that they look for giant breakthroughs and ignore the gradual improvements that occur in real life. Emphasizing small signs of progress can keep your hope alive, even if the overall situation remains challenging:

- **Micro-Goals**: Instead of expecting overnight transformations, set small goals that are easily measured. For example, if you want to heal from a regrettable conflict, a micro-goal might be having one calm conversation without raised voices.
- **Visual Trackers**: Some find it helpful to have a chart or list where they mark each step accomplished. This visible record becomes a daily reminder of forward motion.
- **Praise the Effort**: Even if the outcome is not perfect, acknowledge the effort you invested. Recognizing the attempt encourages you to keep refining your methods.
- **Regular Reflection**: At the end of the week, note what improved, even slightly. This reflection allows you to see a pattern of building momentum, which is vital for sustaining hope when major results have not yet materialized.

When you realize that steady progress is happening, you become less likely to abandon your aims or succumb to regrets. The daily reinforcement of "I am moving, even if slowly" keeps the hopeful spark alive.

---

8. Aligning Hope with Authentic Goals

Sometimes, regrets arise because we chase goals that do not match our deeper values. We might do so out of social pressure or a misguided sense of duty.

When we fail at these inauthentic goals, the regret can be intense. Conversely, maintaining hope is easier if your goals genuinely reflect who you are:

- **Self-Assessment**: Periodically ask if your main objectives align with your core beliefs. Are you striving for a high-paying job only because others expect it, or because it resonates with you? If not, adjust accordingly to prevent future regrets.
- **Value-Based Planning**: Plan steps that honor what you hold important—family, creativity, service, adventure, etc. Hope grows naturally when you see your efforts as true to your identity.
- **Check Past Regrets**: Look at regrets tied to certain ambitions. Did they come from chasing a path that was never really yours? If so, let that regret guide you to a more genuine direction.
- **Measure Success Differently**: Instead of comparing achievements to external benchmarks, measure how well your actions mirror your values. This shift in perspective often reveals that you have reasons for hope, even if you have not met society's definition of success.

Authentic goals provide more stable motivation, reducing the chance of feeling that your efforts are pointless. They feed hope because you sense that each step aligns with who you truly want to be, thereby diminishing regrets born from living someone else's dream.

9. Balancing Hope with Acknowledgment of Challenges

Hope does not mean shutting your eyes to difficulties. Rather, it is the engine that keeps you moving despite them. Balancing hope with a realistic view of obstacles allows you to stay motivated without living in denial:

- **Name the Challenge**: If there is a financial shortfall or a health limitation, clearly state it. Hiding it only leads to illusions, which crumble under pressure and cause deeper regrets.
- **Plan Support**: Gather resources—advice, training, or emotional support—to help you overcome the obstacle. Seeing that assistance is available amplifies your sense of hope.
- **Positive Realism**: Acknowledge that some efforts may fail, but they are still attempts that refine your approach. This balanced stance keeps you from giving up when one plan falters.

By holding both the challenge and the path forward in mind, you keep hope grounded in facts. This approach helps you adapt to setbacks without losing the faith that improvement remains possible.

10. Finding Inspiration from Role Models

Role models who overcame regret or overcame major setbacks can remind you that hope is not just a fantasy. Biographies, interviews, or personal encounters with such individuals can help:

- **Varied Examples**: Look for people from different fields—sports, arts, sciences—who faced serious missteps or adversity. Their journeys often show how determination and vision can triumph over initial failures.
- **Identify Similarities**: Notice details in their stories that match your own situation. Maybe they also felt they started too late or lacked support initially. Recognizing parallels fuels hope that your path can also yield progress.
- **Adapt Their Strategies**: If you see a role model overcame regret by disciplined planning or seeking mentors, try those tactics yourself. While each life story is unique, certain strategies have broad usefulness.
- **Stay Balanced**: Avoid idolizing them to the point of feeling inadequate. The point is to see that flawed humans can still grow, not to compare your real life to someone else's highlight reel.

In moments of doubt, recalling a role model's perseverance can supply the spark you need to keep believing in your own possibilities.

11. Boosting Hope Through Connection with Others

Hope often rises when we share encouragement with trusted individuals. Loneliness and isolation can breed negative self-talk, while supportive networks remind us that change is possible:

- **Friends and Family**: Communicate your hopes and ask for their insights or cheerleading. Even a short message of "I believe in you" can recharge your motivation.

- **Support Groups**: Finding a community—online or offline—that discusses growth, healing, or skill-building can normalize your struggles. You see that regrets and attempts to move past them are universal experiences.
- **Positive Mentoring**: A mentor who sees your potential can restore hope when you doubt yourself. They can give constructive feedback that clarifies your next steps and highlights your strengths.
- **Reciprocal Support**: Offer hope to others, too. When you help someone see their potential, it reminds you that progress is indeed achievable. This cycle of mutual support nurtures a collective sense of hope.

Through connection, you realize your regrets do not isolate you. Many people face setbacks, and together, you can maintain an environment where hope thrives.

---

12. Avoiding False Hopes and Quick Fixes

Hope can be misdirected if you buy into unrealistic promises or shortcuts—like "get-rich-quick" schemes or untested cures. These illusions can lead to deeper regrets once they collapse:

- **Check Credibility**: Before investing resources or time in a solution, research its track record. Is there evidence it works, or is it just hype?
- **Measure Risk**: If a plan sounds too good to be true, it likely carries hidden risks. True hope does not rely on fantasy but on feasible goals that align with reality.
- **Stay Patient**: Quick fixes are appealing because they promise no discomfort. Real progress usually takes steady effort, which is why balanced hope includes patience.
- **Learn from Setbacks**: If you fell for a false hope once, use that regret as a reminder to be more cautious. It does not mean giving up on hope, just applying it more wisely.

Refining your sense of which opportunities are genuine helps your hope remain durable, instead of crashing each time a fake solution fails. This thoughtful approach keeps regrets in check.

13. Using Mindset Shifts for Sustained Hope

Sometimes a small mental shift can reawaken hope when regrets or discouragement weigh you down. A few mindset adjustments include:

- **From "Obstacle" to "Challenge"**: Replace negative labels with neutral or positive words. Instead of viewing an overdue debt as an insurmountable "disaster," call it a "challenge" that you can approach methodically.
- **From "Failure" to "Lesson"**: A mistake is not the final story. Repeatedly remind yourself that each error holds a lesson, as we discussed. This frames regret as part of a learning process, not an irreversible condemnation.
- **From "I Must" to "I Choose"**: Shifting your language from obligation to choice can restore a sense of agency. "I must fix my finances" can feel oppressive, while "I choose to fix my finances" emphasizes your power.
- **Future Self Visualization**: Briefly imagine a future version of you who has overcome the current regret. Ask what that future self might advise. This technique encourages constructive thinking rather than defeat.

These small tweaks help break a negative loop in your head. They keep your focus on possibility rather than on the past.

---

14. Handling Doubt from Past Disappointments

If you have tried to change before and failed, you might feel that hope is an illusion. However, repeated failure can be a learning ground if approached carefully:

- **Identify Specific Flaws in Past Attempts**: Maybe you lacked support or tried unrealistic timelines. Correcting these specifics can improve your new efforts.
- **Acknowledge Skill Growth**: Even if the outcome was not what you wanted, you likely gained new insights or sharpened certain skills. Recognize these small increments of progress.
- **Attempt Fresh Angles**: If your old approach was too narrow, explore alternative paths. A different job, new study method, or fresh location could solve roadblocks that stymied you before.

Reframing past disappointments as incomplete tries rather than total defeats sustains the spark of hope that a better plan can succeed if guided by lessons learned.

15. Protecting Hope During Difficult Times

Life can throw curveballs—health crises, natural disasters, sudden layoffs—that intensify regrets or overshadow all positivity. Maintaining hope in such periods is critical:

- **Focus on What Remains**: Instead of only seeing what is lost, identify the resources still available—health, supportive friends, or intangible qualities like determination. This perspective counters feelings of total devastation.
- **Break Down the New Crisis**: Use problem-solving tactics (as covered in Chapter 17) to tackle urgent needs step by step. Each success in dealing with difficulties reaffirms that improvement is possible.
- **Use Coping Rituals**: Activities like journaling, prayer (if that suits your beliefs), or quiet walks help process emotions without drowning in them. This emotional processing preserves a channel for hopeful thoughts.
- **Seek External Assistance**: Sometimes professional help—emotional or financial—can provide the scaffolding you need to keep hope afloat. Reaching out for help is not weakness; it is a practical move to stabilize your situation.

When storms pass, the fact that you kept any spark of hope alive can fuel gratitude (a separate, beneficial emotion) and further reduce regrets about how you managed the crisis.

16. Turning Hope into Tangible Steps

Hope flourishes when linked to action. Merely feeling hopeful without doing anything can slip into daydreaming. To keep hope effective, ensure it drives concrete moves:

- **Set Clear Goals**: Write them down. If your regret involves missed educational opportunities, set a timeframe for signing up for a course or gathering scholarship information.
- **Include Accountability**: Tell a friend or family member about your plan so they can check in. Accountability keeps hope from fading into complacency.
- **Schedule Milestones**: A big goal might be months away, so plan small tasks each week that move you closer. This steadiness helps you see real progress, reinforcing hope.
- **Adjust as Needed**: If you hit a snag, tweak the plan rather than quitting. This flexibility is how hope remains dynamic. You do not give up; you adapt.

By turning hope into a structured approach, you reduce the risk of drifting. Your daily tasks become evidence that you still see a valuable future and are prepared to work toward it.

---

17. Sustaining Hope Over the Long Haul

Maintaining hope is not just about quick bursts of inspiration. Life is long, and regrets can resurface. These strategies help sustain hope across months or years:

- **Regular Self-Check**: Schedule intervals—monthly, quarterly—to gauge your mental and emotional state. Are regrets creeping back in? Is your sense of possibility faltering? Early detection lets you reinforce hope before it erodes significantly.
- **Evolve Goals**: As you change, your aims shift. Embrace this evolution. Clinging to an outdated dream can cause frustration and regrets. Adapting your goals keeps hope relevant.
- **Surround Yourself with Growth**: Keep reading, learning, meeting people who challenge you in healthy ways. A dynamic environment stops the stagnation that fuels despair.
- **Practice Gratitude**: While different from hope, gratitude can heighten your awareness of what is going well, preventing regrets from dominating your outlook. Spend a moment each day listing what you appreciate, even if small.

When hope is woven into your life structure—through check-ins, evolving aims, and a supportive context—you become far less likely to be derailed by regrets. You have a steady platform for resilience.

18. Conclusion of Chapter 18

Maintaining hope in daily life is a critical defense against the paralyzing weight of regret. Rather than erasing past errors or ignoring reality, hope acknowledges the challenges while holding onto the belief that improvements are within reach. By embracing realistic goals, surrounding yourself with supportive networks, and celebrating small victories, you transform regrets from insurmountable burdens into stepping stones toward growth.

Hope is not a final destination but an ongoing process. It thrives on daily habits—like focusing on small wins, managing cynicism, and aligning your efforts with genuine values. It also deepens when you see regrets as teachers rather than life sentences. Though setbacks and doubts will appear, a hopeful mindset channels your energy into problem-solving and personal development rather than endless rumination on what went wrong. Over time, nurturing hope fosters emotional resilience and helps you engage with life's possibilities, free from the chains of regret's gloom.

CHAPTER 19: SUSTAINING PROGRESS WITHOUT BACKSLIDING

Regret often fades once we correct our behavior or fix a situation. However, maintaining these positive changes is not always easy. If we are not careful, old habits and unhelpful ways of thinking can return. This can lead to a cycle of progress followed by relapse, generating renewed regret. In this chapter, we explore how to sustain forward movement without returning to the patterns that caused regret in the past. We will look at practical steps to keep momentum, address hidden pitfalls, and solidify each gained benefit so that regret becomes less likely to appear again.

1. Why Backsliding Happens

Progress is rarely a straight line. Stress, distraction, or unfamiliar challenges can cause us to lose sight of our improvements and slide back into previous routines. Even positive changes require regular upkeep. For example, if you have established healthier communication with a friend, a single intense argument might revert you to your old style of harsh words. This backsliding can spark renewed regret and the disheartening feeling that no real change was made.

Several factors commonly lead to relapse into old habits:

- **Lack of Reinforcement**: Without a continuous reminder of why you changed in the first place, it is easy to slip back to the default approach.
- **Unrealistic Goals**: If the improvements you aimed for were too large or unsustainable, setbacks become more probable.
- **Environmental Triggers**: Certain situations or people might remind you of past behaviors, nudging you to repeat them.
- **Complacency**: After some success, you might think the problem is solved, and you stop practicing the habits that secured your progress. Old patterns can sneak back.

Recognizing these risks early allows you to plan defenses, ensuring your progress stands firm over time.

2. Setting Up a Personal Maintenance Plan

Sustaining improvement involves more than a single effort; it requires an ongoing plan. This plan reminds you of why you made the change, how you got there, and what steps will prevent slipping backward. An effective personal maintenance plan has these parts:

1. **Clear Definition of the Change**: For example, if you once regretted being distant from loved ones, your new habit might be a weekly call or visit. Write it out: "I will contact my mother every Sunday evening for 15 minutes."
2. **List of Key Motivations**: Note why this matters. Maybe you do not want to revisit the guilt of ignoring family. Include practical benefits—deeper bonds, fewer conflicts—so that your brain stays focused on the positive impact.
3. **Schedule for Regular Check-Ins**: Every so often (weekly, monthly), reflect on whether you maintained the new habit. If you missed a step, ask why and correct it immediately, before a small lapse becomes a complete return to old ways.
4. **Back-Up Strategies**: Identify what you will do if you feel unmotivated or encounter stress. If your new habit is daily exercise, but you feel tired, your back-up might be a light stretching session rather than skipping all activity.

A maintenance plan gives structure, so your new behaviors are not based on fleeting motivation but on consistent reminders and strategies.

3. Turning Changes into Part of Your Identity

One method to prevent backsliding is to integrate your new habit or mindset into your core self-image. Rather than seeing the change as a short-term fix, view it as part of who you are now. For instance, if you previously regretted poor money management and you have begun budgeting well, you could describe yourself as "a responsible budgeter" or "someone who wisely handles finances." This identity shift can strengthen commitment and reduce the urge to fall back. When you think, "This is who I am," straying from the new pattern feels unnatural.

To deepen this identity:

- **Positive Self-Talk**: Each time you successfully practice the new behavior, quietly note to yourself, "This confirms I am a person who does [X]."
- **Public Acknowledgment**: If appropriate, share this aspect of your identity with supportive friends. Saying "I'm focused on maintaining good finances

these days" can keep you accountable and embed the change in your social interactions.
- **Rituals and Symbols**: For certain types of improvements, a small symbol can represent your new identity. It might be a daily check on an app that tracks progress, or a wristband that reminds you of your commitment. Repeated exposure to these signals cements the habit as part of you.

This approach transforms the improvement from an external rule to an internal, natural preference.

4. Avoiding Overconfidence After Early Success

A common reason for returning to old habits is overconfidence. Once we see some good results—maybe we overcame a major regret or handled a conflict well—we can assume we have solved the underlying issue. But real change is not only about short-term wins. Overconfidence can make us drop the habits that created success, thinking we no longer need them. This sets us up for a slow drift back into previous patterns.

- **Stay Humble**: Recognize that each day requires attention. Even highly disciplined individuals keep checklists or reminders to stay on track. Humility in this sense means admitting that your past ways can resurface if you get complacent.
- **Keep Reviewing Goals**: Do not discard your written goals or references just because you made progress. Return to them periodically, even if you believe you have "mastered" the new habit. This keeps your mind from neglecting important details.
- **Plan for Plateaus**: Progress might stall. You might not see big leaps as you did at the start. In these periods, keep practicing. The fact that you are not backsliding is itself a success. Overconfidence can be replaced by consistent effort, ensuring that slow periods do not cause you to lose interest.

By staying modest about your improvements, you leave space for continuous growth and prevent the pride that often leads to falling back into old mistakes.

5. The Role of Environment in Holding Gains

Your surroundings can either help or hurt your drive to maintain a new standard. If your environment constantly brings up triggers linked to your old behavior, it is more likely you will slip. Consider these steps to optimize your physical and social environment:

- **Physical Layout**: For example, if you regret overspending and want to adopt better budgeting, keep financial tracking items (like a budget notebook) in a place you see daily. Likewise, avoid leaving credit cards in easily accessible spots if impulse shopping is your downfall.
- **Social Circle**: Evaluate whether certain friends or relatives encourage old habits. If your aim is to quit harmful habits, being around those who constantly do those activities can undermine your progress. You might need to explain your stance or reduce time spent in those circles if they do not respect your changes.
- **Supportive Cues**: Introduce reminders—posters, phone alerts, or a shared calendar with a friend—to strengthen your new habits. The more your environment nudges you in a helpful direction, the less mental energy you spend resisting old ways.

Shaping the environment is not about hiding from reality but about lowering the friction for good habits and increasing the friction for harmful ones. This practical measure often makes the difference between steady growth and relapse.

6. Handling Periodic Urges or Temporary Slips

Even the most thorough maintenance plan does not remove every urge. You might occasionally feel drawn back toward the behavior or mindset you left behind. A single slip—a missed weekly call or an angry outburst—does not have to destroy your progress unless you let it. Dealing with minor setbacks effectively helps stop a small mistake from snowballing into a full return to regretful conduct.

- **Normalize Occasional Discomfort**: Understand that occasional pull toward the old habit is natural. It does not prove your improvement is fake. The real test is how you respond.
- **Use Quick Recovery Steps**: If you lose your temper once, apologize promptly and revisit your conflict-resolution plan. If you skip a workout, resume the routine the next day without beating yourself up. Quick corrections show your mind that a slip is not a reason to give up entirely.
- **Reflect Without Harshness**: Ask yourself what triggered the slip. Were you tired, stressed, or around a certain person? Turn the slip into a

chance to refine your approach, maybe by changing your environment or planning more rest.

By treating urges and slips as normal, you lessen the emotional weight of a small error and keep it from turning into a spiral of renewed regret.

7. Accountability Partnerships and Ongoing Feedback

Sometimes the difference between holding onto progress and sliding backwards is having an accountability partner. This could be a close friend, a mentor, or a group that supports each other's goals. The idea is simple: you report your progress to them, and they offer encouragement or caution as needed. Knowing that someone will check in about your new habit can raise your sense of responsibility.

- **Weekly Check-Ins**: A brief call or message exchange can keep your focus sharp. You share any challenges or close calls, and your partner can remind you of your original motivation.
- **Exchange Feedback**: If they notice you returning to certain behaviors or language that signals old patterns, they can point it out early. Likewise, you can do the same for them if it is a mutual arrangement.
- **Group Settings**: Sometimes entire groups form around maintaining specific improvements—like sobriety, healthy eating, or improved communication. A structured group might have guidelines for meeting frequency and ways to share successes or concerns.
- **Positive Reinforcement**: When you do well, your accountability partner can offer a sincere "Well done." Such feedback is not the forbidden word we must avoid; it simply acknowledges your effort. Acknowledgment from someone else is a potent force to keep you on track.

Accountability is not about shame or policing each other. It is about mutual support, which can be a powerful tool against returning to old regret patterns.

8. Integrating New Habits into Various Life Areas

To truly lock in your progress, go beyond the narrow scope of the original change and spread elements of the improved behavior into multiple life areas. For instance, if you improved your budgeting skills, you might apply the same principles of planning and careful research to other domains—like scheduling your time better or analyzing major decisions more thoroughly. This cross-application turns the improvement into a broad skill rather than a single fix.

Examples:

- **Communication Techniques**: If you stopped harsh arguments in your home life, try using calmer communication at work. The more you see it working in varied settings, the stronger it becomes.
- **Self-Reflection**: If journaling about regrets has helped you handle your personal life, maybe journaling about workplace issues can prevent conflicts there as well.
- **Time Management Gains**: Suppose you overcame a regret about never finishing tasks on time. Now you can apply these scheduling and prioritizing tactics to your personal projects, hobbies, or volunteer roles. Each success in a new environment cements the habit more deeply.

By spreading your updated practices to different corners of your life, you ensure they are not confined to just one context. This broad usage acts like extra layers of reinforcement, making backsliding less likely.

9. Watching Out for Hidden Triggers and Complacency

Sometimes, progress unravels not because of obvious obstacles but due to small, hidden triggers that push you off track slowly. It might be the subtle stress of a new job role, the quiet tension in a relationship, or a minor health issue draining your energy. These unrecognized factors can wear away at your focus, causing you to revert to old ways.

- **Periodic Self-Assessment**: Every month or so, do a quick scan: "Am I feeling new sources of stress? Have my routines shifted in a way that might threaten my new habit?" Being proactive helps you spot trouble early.
- **Emotional Signals**: Pay attention if you notice renewed frustration, sadness, or anxiety in your daily life. These signals might indicate a growing mismatch between your environment and the behaviors you want to maintain. Investigate and address the cause before it triggers a full relapse.
- **Update Strategies**: As life evolves, your plan to maintain changes must also adapt. For instance, if your schedule becomes busier, you may need to streamline your new habit to fit the time constraints instead of abandoning it.

Anticipating subtle shifts ensures you do not wake up one morning back at square one, wondering how you slipped so far from your improved state.

10. Strengthening Internal Motivation

External motives—like avoiding public shame or meeting others' expectations—can spark initial change. But for lasting progress, internal motivation is far more stable. Shoring up your internal drive helps keep you from relapsing when external pressure fades.

- **Tie Changes to Personal Values**: Ask how each improvement resonates with your deeper beliefs. If you see it supports honesty, responsibility, or kindness—values that matter to you—you are more likely to defend it against lapses.
- **Evolve Your Goals**: Let your goals grow along with you. If a certain target is no longer challenging or relevant, shift it. Keeping goals fresh prevents boredom and fosters ongoing commitment.
- **Self-Reward Structures**: Small self-given acknowledgments of effort can keep you motivated. This does not mean lavish celebrations but maybe something modest like taking a short break or enjoying a favorite (reasonable) treat each time you complete a set stage of the new habit.
- **Reflect on the Cost of Old Regrets**: Remember how you felt before you changed. The memory of that regret can reinforce why you never want to return to that place.

Self-driven changes are less vulnerable to external fluctuations, making them more robust over time.

11. Becoming a Resource for Others

When you maintain a positive change, your story can inspire others who face similar regrets. Taking on a guiding role can also reinforce your progress because teaching and mentorship keep you focused on what worked. By advising others:

- **You Re-Teach Yourself**: Sharing advice solidifies the lessons in your own mind. If you drift from your own advice, you will spot the contradiction quickly.
- **Increased Accountability**: People look to you as an example, so you have more reason to stay consistent.

- **Expanded Perspective**: Helping others might reveal angles or questions that you never considered. This broadens your understanding and resilience against future setbacks.

However, be mindful not to overreach or preach. Offer guidance humbly, staying aware that you, too, are still on a path of continued practice.

12. Celebrating Milestones Responsibly

Although we are avoiding the forbidden word for "celebrate," we can still highlight the importance of marking milestones without letting our guard down. Reaching 30 days of not returning to a bad habit, or a year of improved budgeting, is an achievement. Recognizing such benchmarks can be motivational. The key is to do it in a way that does not encourage complacency.

- **Low-Risk Activities**: If you overcame a regret involving substance use, do not mark a milestone by indulging in triggers. Instead, pick an activity that supports well-being—like visiting a scenic spot or cooking a healthy meal with friends.
- **Public Acknowledgment**: Sometimes sharing your milestone in a group that understands your struggle offers a morale boost. Positive community feedback can increase your determination.
- **Reflect Rather Than Party**: Focus on reflecting how you succeeded, what made it possible, and what you can improve next. This reflection underscores your achievements while reinforcing a forward-looking mindset.

By framing milestones as checkpoints instead of final endings, you keep building on your progress instead of letting down your guard.

13. Balancing Stability with Willingness to Evolve

Maintaining change does not mean locking yourself into the exact same routine forever. It is about preserving the core improvements while staying flexible to new conditions. If your life context shifts—a move to a new city, a relationship status change, or a health variation—you might need to tweak your approach.

- **Foundation vs. Adaptation**: Keep the basic principles that made your transformation possible. For example, if careful daily planning reduced your regrets, keep scheduling your tasks. But adapt the details to fit new job hours or living arrangements.

- **Open to Feedback**: Regularly ask yourself or trusted friends, "Is my strategy still working well? Are we seeing any signs of old patterns returning?" This prompt helps you know if new tweaks are needed.
- **Self-Awareness of Growth**: As you gain experience, your perspective might shift. The version of you who started this process might have had simpler targets. Now you might aim higher or approach problems with greater nuance. Let that growth guide updates to your plan.

Striking a balance between consistent upkeep and readiness to adjust ensures your changes remain alive and aligned with your evolving life.

14. Avoiding All-or-Nothing Thinking

One subtle trap that fuels backsliding is the mindset that if you fail once, all is lost. This black-and-white view can turn a single misstep into a reason to abandon all progress. But real improvement is a range, not a perfection test.

- **Graded Success**: If you are 80% better than before, that is still a major success even if not perfect. A single mistake might reduce you to 75% for a day, but it does not have to be 0%.
- **Reset Quickly**: Remind yourself: "I made one error, but I am still far ahead of where I was." Then resume your improved behavior right away. This stops the downward spiral.
- **Praise Partial Wins**: Recognize partial wins. For instance, if your new goal was to manage anger, but you only partially succeeded in a tense moment, you might have used calmer words but still raised your voice at the end. That partial success indicates growth, even if not perfect.

This approach respects that human change seldom arrives in pure extremes. By moving beyond all-or-nothing thinking, you keep one stumble from erasing months of effort.

15. Monitoring Your Mindset Through Ongoing Reflection

Sustaining change is not only about external habits. Your mindset—your beliefs, assumptions, and attitudes—shapes how stable that change remains. Ongoing reflection helps you notice if your thoughts start leaning back toward old beliefs that once fueled regret.

- **Daily or Weekly Journal**: Write a brief entry about your emotional state, achievements, or annoyances. Patterns might emerge if negativity or defeatist thinking returns.
- **Check Core Beliefs**: If you overcame a regret about feeling unworthy, watch for signs that you are telling yourself "I am worthless" again. Replace that with evidence of your growth.
- **Course Correction**: If old negative thoughts appear, apply the mental exercises that worked before—positive affirmations, reframing your perspective, or focusing on new facts that counter your old assumptions.

By tracking your mental climate, you reduce the chance that hidden negativity will quietly erode your progress and lead to fresh regrets.

16. Planning for Long-Term Integration

The final aim is to have your new behaviors or attitudes so deeply woven into your life that you no longer see them as "extra tasks." They become second nature. While the process can be lengthy, the payoff is a life largely free from the regrets that once haunted you.

- **Stretch Your Vision**: Picture yourself 5 or 10 years from now living these improved habits as your normal routine. Such envisioning can reinforce your daily commitment.
- **Set Progressive Goals**: Every time you stabilize one level of change, set a slightly higher aim. If you fixed your finances at a basic level, now try investing wisely or planning for retirement. Growth fosters momentum and wards off boredom.
- **Review Milestones Over Time**: Each year, reflect on where you started and how far you have come. This reflection helps you see that the new normal is rooted in real achievements, not an unstable experiment.
- **Stay Aware of New Sources of Regret**: Over the long term, life changes can produce different regrets. Applying the strategies from this entire book can help you handle new regrets without losing the ground you already gained.

Long-term integration is not a final finish line but a lifestyle that weaves consistent self-awareness and adjustment into your daily existence.

17. Finding Satisfaction in the Present

It is tempting to always look to the future or measure if you have truly outrun your old regrets. While forward focus is crucial, do not forget to find satisfaction in your present achievements. Recognizing your day-to-day sense of self can protect you from the anxious feeling that you are never "doing enough."

- **Mindful Appreciation**: Pause occasionally and take note of small improvements in your daily life: a calmer argument, a better meal plan, a stable mood at work. Let yourself enjoy these successes without overshadowing them with concerns about tomorrow.
- **Avoid Endless Comparison**: If you keep comparing your progress to others or to some ideal standard, you might undermine your sense of accomplishment. Focus on your own path and notice that each day of stable improvement is a personal victory.
- **Release Guilt Over Past**: Guilt about old regrets can overshadow current achievements. Remind yourself that part of growth is allowing yourself to accept that you have changed. It is okay to find peace in your new habits.

Balanced contentment in the present helps your new behaviors flourish by giving you a sense of stability and satisfaction. That sense of peace wards off the anxiety that can prompt relapse or new regrets.

18. Conclusion of Chapter 19

Sustaining progress without backsliding is a dynamic, ongoing process that demands attention to habits, environment, mindset, and self-awareness. While regret can fade once you take steps toward improvement, the real test comes after those first victories. Avoiding overconfidence, shaping your environment to support rather than undermine you, and having clear strategies for slip-ups are crucial. Regular reflection and accountability help you catch early signs of backsliding, while adopting new behaviors as part of your identity strengthens your commitment.

This chapter has shown that real change is not a quick fix but an integrated approach. It involves turning each improvement into a natural part of your daily routines, keeping watch for potential threats, and adjusting to life's evolving conditions. By maintaining your progress, you ensure that old regrets remain in the past, and you build the confidence to handle new challenges that arise. In the next and final chapter, we will look at broader reflections on regret, and how to plan for a future that leaves less room for regret to take root again.

CHAPTER 20: FINAL REFLECTIONS AND FUTURE OUTLOOK

As we arrive at the closing chapter of "How to Overcome Regret: Understanding, Accepting, and Moving On," it is useful to assemble the core insights from the previous sections and turn them toward the road ahead. This book has shown that regret, while painful, is also a window into our deeper values and a prompt for constructive change. When used wisely, regret can reveal flaws in our thinking or behavior, pushing us to strengthen our problem-solving skills, our emotional management, and our relationships. Yet regret's negative impact can linger unless we approach it with clear strategies: acceptance, learning, consistent application of better habits, and a forward-focused sense of hope.

Here, we bring together final reflections that highlight how to integrate everything into a cohesive perspective on life, so that regret does not overshadow your future opportunities. We will also consider ways to remain flexible, open, and ready for new possibilities. By blending these elements, you can face each new day with confidence and use your past regrets as stepping stones, not anchors that weigh you down.

1. Recognizing the Arc of Growth

Every story of self-improvement contains highs and lows, breakthroughs, and unexpected setbacks. Seeing your life as a broader progression helps give context to any regretful events that happened along the way. You are not defined by a single mistake, nor are you purely the sum of your best moments. Instead, you are evolving.

- **Comparing Early and Recent Actions**: If you once struggled with certain regrets, reflect on how you would handle the same scenario now. Even subtle differences in your approach can mark real progress.
- **Maintaining Perspective**: Changes in personal growth rarely happen overnight. Remember that an arc with small upward trends still forms a positive direction, even if some dips occur.
- **Embracing Complexity**: Accept complexity. You can feel regret over a specific choice, yet still acknowledge that it added knowledge or relationships to your life that you value. Human life is often a blend of positive and negative outcomes from the same events.

Recognizing growth as a layered process frees you from the trap of labeling yourself solely by regret. Each stage you pass through adds depth to your understanding and ability to handle future trials.

2. Reviewing What Regret Has Taught You

At this point, you likely see regret differently than you did at the start of this book. Instead of viewing it merely as a painful emotion, you might now see it as a clue about what you care about most, a teacher that pinpoints areas needing attention, or even a motivator for personal expansion. Summarize what you have learned from your regrets:

- **Reevaluate Priorities**: Did your regrets show you that you prize family more than you realized? Or that financial security is more urgent than you admitted? Pinpoint these revelations so you can align future decisions accordingly.
- **Enhance Empathy**: Regret sometimes arises from harming others or failing to support them. This painful realization can deepen your empathy. You might now better understand how certain words or actions affect those around you.
- **Develop Self-Trust**: If you addressed a regret and fixed the underlying issue, your confidence in your capacity for change grows. Remember that success story when facing new hurdles.
- **Refine Boundaries**: Some regrets come from letting people cross our boundaries or from crossing theirs. Understanding where those lines should stand can help you form healthier relationships and avoid repeated sorrow.

These insights serve as a personal "manual" of sorts—a reference you can consult when facing uncertainty or new dilemmas.

3. Embracing Ongoing Self-Awareness

Welcoming ongoing self-awareness is a vital conclusion to the entire process. It is not enough to realize you can handle regret productively; you also must monitor your thoughts and actions to catch new regrets before they grow large. Self-awareness acts like an early warning system:

- **Daily Quiet Time**: Even five minutes of reflection—mental or in a journal—can help you spot small worries or incomplete tasks that might soon become regrets if ignored.

- **Listen to Your Emotions**: If you find yourself unusually tense or defensive, ask yourself what is causing it. Is there a fear of repeating a past mistake? Is a relationship dynamic causing concern?
- **Remain Curious**: Approach your own behavior with curiosity rather than judgment. Instead of quickly deciding "I messed up again," ask, "What is driving this behavior? Do I see parallels with a past regret?"
- **Adopt Corrective Measures Early**: If you see a potential regret forming, intervene. That might mean clarifying a misunderstanding, setting a boundary, or reevaluating a decision. Prompt action can save you from bigger regrets.

Self-awareness is not about constant self-criticism. Rather, it is a gentle, regular scan that helps you steer your life in a direction that matches your values and lessens the chance of regrets.

4. Building a Regret-Resistant Future

While no one can eliminate all regrets, you can shape your decisions to reduce the likelihood of major remorse. A "regret-resistant" future involves preemptive thinking and robust personal strategies:

- **Risk-Benefit Analysis**: Before big choices—whether financial, emotional, or lifestyle-based—assess not only short-term thrills but also the long-term cost if it goes wrong. This approach requires patience, but it drastically cuts down on impulsive regrets.
- **Goal Setting with Flexibility**: Having goals can give you structure. However, keep them flexible so that if a new path emerges or unforeseen hurdles appear, you can shift course rather than feeling locked into a plan that no longer fits. Rigidity often creates regret when life changes.
- **Healthy Support System**: Surround yourself with people who encourage thoughtful action and honest reflection. Such friends or mentors can gently warn you when they see you leaning toward choices that might yield regret.
- **Regular Skill Development**: As the world evolves, so do the skills needed to navigate it. Keeping your knowledge current—whether that is communication methods, technological tools, or self-care practices—helps you stay adaptable and avoid regrets tied to missed learning.

No strategy grants total immunity from regret, but each of these steps lowers the odds of avoidable mistakes and positions you to handle adversity with clarity.

5. Emphasizing Both Accountability and Kindness

Throughout this book, we have seen that regret often involves two big themes: taking responsibility for our errors and treating ourselves with understanding. Neither alone is enough. Without accountability, we avoid owning our mistakes, which makes personal growth unlikely. Without kindness, we drown in self-blame that can lock us into the very patterns we wish to change.

- **Balance in Practice**: When a regret surfaces, accept your part in what went wrong, then apply supportive strategies—like reframing or seeking counsel—to move on. This mixture of honesty and compassion fosters real maturity.
- **Open Apologies**: If your regret concerns hurting another person, be bold enough to apologize. Yet remain kind to yourself, remembering you are capable of redemption and better conduct in the future.
- **Transform Blame into Improvement**: Instead of dwelling on how foolish you were, direct that mental energy into tangible steps. Ask, "What specific lesson can I take from this so it does not recur?" That forward shift is part accountability, part self-kindness.

This balanced stance helps you keep regrets in a constructive space, ensuring they push you toward self-improvement instead of self-punishment.

6. Accepting That Some Regrets Cannot Be Fixed

Some regrets may not have perfect solutions. You might not be able to restore a lost relationship or regain an opportunity that slipped by. Acknowledging this finality can be painful, but resisting it does not undo the situation. Accepting the limitation frees you to do what you can in the present:

- **Partial Closure**: If you cannot fix the entire outcome, see if a smaller act might bring closure. Perhaps you cannot contact a deceased loved one to apologize, but you can write a letter expressing your thoughts, read it aloud privately, and then set it aside.
- **Direct Efforts Elsewhere**: Channel the regret's lesson into your current relationships or tasks. Let the memory fuel more attentive behavior so the same regret does not repeat in a new context.
- **Release Unrealistic Fantasies**: Holding onto the idea of fully reversing time can trap you in heartbreak. Recognize that letting go of an impossible fix is a form of healing, not a betrayal of the person or the missed chance.

- **Finding Value Despite Pain**: Even regrets that cannot be resolved can deepen your perspective on life. They can highlight precious truths about love, responsibility, or timing. That wisdom can color your future decisions in a positive way.

When a regret truly resists repair, acceptance may be the only route to peace. Though not easy, it is a step of emotional maturity that allows you to keep living without carrying an endless burden of blame.

7. Sustaining a Flexible Vision for the Future

Regret often ties to goals that did not happen or events that went wrong. One way to remain hopeful and resilient is to maintain a flexible vision of the future. That does not mean you have no plans, but rather that you keep them adaptable:

- **Plan with Options**: Instead of a rigid one-track blueprint, prepare a plan A and a plan B. If a certain career path or relocation does not work out, you already have an alternate route in mind. This readiness lowers the heartbreak if your first choice falls through.
- **Adjust to Changing Interests**: You might discover new passions later in life. Rather than seeing your old plan as a sign you must remain on a path you no longer love, grant yourself permission to pivot. Some regrets arise from ignoring fresh interests to stick rigidly to old promises.
- **Incorporate Emotional Safety Nets**: Keep enough emotional and practical resources—like savings, close friends, or a healthy coping routine—to handle surprises. This backup makes you less likely to face big regrets when life throws a curveball.

A flexible future outlook means you stay prepared for the unexpected and can adapt your course without feeling that you failed just because you changed direction.

8. Choosing Continuous Improvement Over Perfection

Regret can sometimes push people into a perfectionist mindset, trying to ensure they never make another mistake. But that can lead to constant stress. Instead, focus on steady improvements while accepting that total perfection is not realistic.

- **Progress Checkpoints**: Measure yourself by your own previous state. Compare how you handle disagreements now versus a year ago, not by some flawless ideal that no real person reaches.

- **Smaller, Doable Steps**: Take incremental actions that raise your skill or knowledge over time. This approach builds confidence without the pressure to do everything flawlessly at once.
- **Acknowledge Growth**: You might still slip up, but if you fix issues faster or see them coming sooner, that alone is progress. Each partial success reduces the scope of regret.
- **Healthy Self-Talk**: Replace statements like "I must never mess up" with "I will keep learning and improving." This gentler directive fosters better outcomes long term.

Pursuing continuous improvement keeps regrets manageable by letting each mistake feed into your growth cycle instead of fueling destructive self-criticism.

9. Nurturing Hope as a Lifelong Attitude

Hope has surfaced in multiple chapters as the antidote to despair, discouragement, and the inertia that can follow regret. Maintaining a hopeful mindset over a lifetime adds resilience against any regrets that might emerge in the future. It means you anticipate that there is usually a route forward, even if it is not the one you initially imagined.

- **Collect Examples of Overcoming**: Keep stories or memories of times you overcame tough odds. Refer back to them when a new challenge looms or a new regret threatens to paralyze you.
- **Hope-Filled Surroundings**: Whether it is books, friends, or simple affirmations, keep signals of positivity in your daily life. This ensures your environment remains a source of encouragement.
- **Help Others See Hope**: When you support loved ones in their times of regret, you also reinforce your own hopeful stance. Seeing them respond to your encouragement can remind you that transformation is within reach for everyone.

Hope, when balanced with realism, lets you face regrets with an active spirit. You know difficulties are real, but you also know new possibilities are real as well.

10. Crafting a Personal Regret Philosophy

After working through the processes in this book, you can form your own approach to regrets—like a personal "regret philosophy." It might include principles like:

- "I will own my mistakes without labeling myself as beyond help."
- "I will use regret as a lesson plan, turning each instance into guidance for better decisions."
- "I will apologize quickly when my regrets involve others, aiming for healing rather than shame."
- "I will keep my future open to revision, ensuring regrets do not chain me to old patterns."

Writing out or mentally storing this mini-manifesto can serve as your guiding star whenever regrets threaten to control your thoughts.

11. Creating Room for New Joy

It is easy to become so focused on avoiding regrets that you forget to explore what brings genuine joy. Life is not only about preventing negative outcomes; it is also about finding activities, relationships, and achievements that fill you with satisfaction. Freeing up mental space from old regrets allows you to discover or deepen experiences that make life worthwhile.

- **Schedule Fun**: Plan time for hobbies, social gatherings, or relaxation. This helps you maintain a healthy mental state and counters the gloom that can stem from regretful memories.
- **Experiment with Passions**: Try new pursuits that spark your curiosity. Even if you do not become an expert, the act of exploring can awaken excitement.
- **Allow Real Connection**: If past regrets made you guarded in relationships, gently open yourself to friendships or deeper conversations. Seeking joy in human bonds helps heal old wounds.

When your life includes a positive dimension—sources of contentment, laughter, creativity—you build a natural buffer against regrets overshadowing everything else.

12. Final Thoughts on Going Forward

Regret might always be possible, but you now have many tools to handle it well and prevent it from dominating your mindset. By combining acceptance, self-compassion, structured problem-solving, accountability, flexible planning, and an ongoing sense of hope, you create a lifestyle that respects past lessons without being chained to them. Each step you have taken in this book strengthens the foundation of your everyday living. The aim is not to erase history, but to allow it to inform, refine, and guide you toward a more thoughtful, resilient, and fulfilled future.

Practical Next Steps

- **Regularly Revisit Key Chapters**: If you feel stuck or sense old regrets resurfacing, go back to the relevant sections of this book (like problem-solving, emotional self-care, or building hope). Each part offers specific techniques you can reapply.
- **Stay Connected**: Do not isolate yourself. If regrets return or new ones appear, talk to trusted friends, mentors, or professionals. They can remind you of your progress and help you find fresh approaches.
- **Adapt Principles to Your Reality**: Tailor the ideas you learned here to your culture, personality, and environment. Pick what resonates strongly and refine it to suit your changing circumstances.
- **Keep Evolving**: As you grow older or face major life transitions, new regrets could come up. But the method—accept, understand, strategize, move forward—remains the same. Each time, you will be more prepared than before.

13. Conclusion of Chapter 20

You have traveled through a comprehensive exploration of regret—its causes, its emotional weight, and its potential to teach us. Along the way, you gained tools for analysis, emotional management, relationship repair, hope-building, and sustained progress. The power to handle regret is now in your hands. Although life will keep presenting unexpected twists, you have a strong foundation for meeting them without being trapped by remorse.

Remember that any regret, large or small, can serve as a turning point. By spotting it early, taking responsibility with kindness, and applying the strategies covered in these chapters, you transform regret from a source of pain into a prompt for growth. The final aim is not to attain a life utterly free of mistakes—that is impossible—but to cultivate a mindset and routine that stops mistakes from defining you. Step by step, you build a future shaped less by regret and more by clarity, adaptability, and genuine self-understanding.

You now hold the insight and resources to continue your life's path with confidence. Mistakes will happen, but they need not lock you into a spiral of shame or missed opportunities.

www.ingramcontent.com/pod-product-compliance
Lightning Source LLC
LaVergne TN
LVHW012106070526
838202LV00056B/5640